CHILD REARING PRACTICES IN TRIBALS

A. KUSUMA
M.Sc., M.Ed., M.Phil., P.G. Dip. in Statistics, Ph.D.

Department of Human Development and Family Studies,
Sri Padmavathi Mahila Visvavidyalayam,
Tirupati (A.P.)

1997

DISCOVERY PUBLISHING HOUSE
NEW DELHI—110 002

First Published—1997

ISBN 81-7141-388-9

© *Author*

Published by :

Discovery Publishing House
4831/24, Ansari Road, Prahlad Street
Darya Ganj, New Delhi—110 002 (INDIA)
Phone : 327 92 45
Fax.: 91-11-3253475

Laser Typeset by :

Allied Computers,
Karnal (Haryana)

Printed at :

Tarun Offset Phone : 2260794

To

MY PARENTS

and

HUSBAND

Foreword

Children are the asset of a nation. A society's civilization is measured on how it protects and cares for its children.

Child rearing may be considered to include the overall care, socialization and training of the growing child in a particular culture.

Although infancy and early childhood occupy a only fraction of entire life span, they are crucial in determining and influencing the course of adult life. Proper foundation laid by parents aids in the promotion of desirable personality development of an individual which is acceptable by the society. As child rearing practices are positively related to subsequent personality development, the practices adopted by the parent become significant in shaping a child's life in every sense of the term.

The process of child rearing is greatly influenced by the characteristic ways of thinking, feeling and acting prevalent in the cultural group to which the family belongs.

India is a vast country with many sets of culture and sub-groups within each cultural group. Therefore, regardless of how child rearing is viewed important aspects of cultural differences between groups make the dimensions of considerations rather wide. In addition, every society has set rules that the growing infant is required to conform to.

There are a few books relating to child rearing practices in tribals with special reference to Sugalis. The author humbly feels that this is a new kind of study in a field which has not been explored adequately so far and hopes that the findings of the study will shed new light in this area.

The book is an endeavour to provide the readers with a comprehensive view on child rearing practices in Sugali tribals. It is an extremely significant work and makes serious contributions to Sociology, Anthropology, Psychology, Home Science, Social Work, Education etc.

This book can be read with advantage by Legislators, policy makers, programme planners, administrators, social workers, psychologists, home scientists, counsellors and teachers. Researchers and students will find this volume provocative and creative.

Prof. A. Satyavathi
Principal
University College
Sri Padmavathi Mahila Visvavidyalayam
Tirupati (Andhra Pradesh)

Acknowledgements

The investigator wishes to express her deep sense of gratitude and appreciation to :

Ms. Anna Mathew, M.Sc., B.Ed., Reader, Department of Home Science, Sri Venkateswara University College of Arts and Sciences, Tirupati, for her guidance, interest and encouragement most generously given at every stage of this work.

Dr. (Ms.) P.R. Reddy, Professor and Ms. N.V. Seshamma, Head, Department of Home Science, S.V. University College of Arts and Sciences, Tirupati for their valuable suggestions and encouragement.

Ms. V. Vijayalakshmi, Statistician, Department of Home Science, S.V. University College of Arts and Sciences, Tirupati for her valuable assistance in expediting the statistical part of this work.

Dr. A. Munirathnam Reddy, Professor and Head of the Department of Social Anthropology, S.V. University College of Arts and Sciences, Tirupati for his constant help and encouragement.

The subjects of the present study for their cooperation and patience in giving information on child rearing practices.

The teaching staff of the Department of Home Science for their help and encouragement.

The friends and well-wishers for their encouragement in successful completion of this work.

A. Kusuma

Contents

1
Introduction

'Child rearing' is a broad concept. It is described by various scholars, to include various tasks with some agreement on what it really includes. Hence it may be considered to include the overall care, socialization and training of the growing child in a particular culture. Thus it may be viewed as the tasks that aid meeting the needs of the growing child, of various stages of the life cycle.

Practices related to child rearing have been topics of interest among Sociologists, Anthropologists, Home Scientists as well as Psychologists and Educationists. However, the interest of the re-searchers of these various disciplines, and their line of thinking have been markedly different. For example, Sociologists and Anthropologists study child rearing practices as explorations in the societal models of operations, as variations in social and cultural milieu of different geographical and climatic regions and as influences of political and other environmental changes on the human being as an individual and as a part of a larger cultural of social group. The Psychologists, on the other hand, study the development of personality and temperament as results of these external environmental influences (Bhogle, S. 1978). The early research in child rearing practices which was mainly undertaken by Sears, R.R., Maccoby, E.E., and Levin, H.R. (1957), Whiting, B.B. and Whiting, J.W.M. (1975) had its basis in social learning theory. It attempted to find the relationship of behaviour patterns of children with the learning environment received through home and parents. It also assumed that the behaviour patterns established in the early formative years of a child will be more or less consistent through the adult life. This line of thinking originated from Freud (1856-1939) and his psychoanalytic school of thought, where Freud emphasized the importance of the early years in the life of an individual child's relationship with the parents.

The age-old saying "child is the father of the man' brings out the important place accorded to child and its proper growth in any society. All parents are interested in their children and employ different methods for bringing them up. The purpose of child rearing are two fold; i) to help the child achieve a personal state of well-being and, ii) to help the child become a productive well-socialized member of society. These are the broad long-term goals of child rearing.

Child rearing practices do not exist in isolation but are usually related to a broader constellation of environmental events. In earlier times people attached little importance to the study of child rearing. now people have become enlightened and a large number of studies have come out in recent years with concurring results and at times with contradictory findings. Child rearing practices are considered as a product of ideas, beliefs and attitudes prevalent in a community on how to bring up children. These ideas are bound to change as a result of global environmental changes. Infact the ideas prevalent on child rearing practices a few decades ago may appear remote and alien to the new generation. Nevertheless, the attitudes of past generation is found to have a greater hold on people than is generally realised. Ideas that one is not conscious of may continue to exert an influence on the levels of less conscious feelings which are transmitted from one generation to the next through the process of child rearing itself. The process of child rearing is greatly influenced by the characteristic ways of thinking, feeling and acting prevalent in the cultural group to which the family belongs.

There is considerable emphasis in literature on the culture in which a child is born determining some typical personality traits which are inherent in every individual of that culture in varying degrees. Cultural traits are acquired, they are not a part of nature.

India is a vast country with many sets of culture, and sub-groups within each cultural groups. Therefore, regardless of how child rearing is viewed, important aspects of cultural differences between groups make the dimensions of considerations rather wide. It addition, every society has some set rules that the growing infant is required to conform to. Each group in turn also differs in techniques that are used for enforcing and reinforcing conformity.

The present enquiry is concerned with the study of the child rearing practices in the Sugali mothers of Andhra Pradesh.

Traditional tribal groups possess certain features which might include the following: (Desai, A.R., 1960).

1) they live away from the civilized world in the most inaccessible parts of forests and hills;

2) they speak a tribal dialect;

3) they profess a primitive religion known as "Animism" in which the worship of ghosts and spirits is the most important element;

4) they follow primitive occupations such as hunting and gathering of forest produce;

5) they are largely meat eaters;

6) they live either naked or semi-naked, using tree barks and leaves for clothing;

7) they have nomadic habits, and

8) they love drink and dance.

After the attainment of independence in 1947, the Government of India has been making consistent effort to bring the tribal population into the mainstream of society. The State Government of Andhra Pradesh like the other States also started colonizing the tribals and inspiring them to become settled agriculturists. But occupational structures of tribals often change depending on their survival needs. However, the traditional tribes have been influenced by the Governmental welfare measures as well as urbanization and industrialization with the result that they are in a state of transition at present.

A vast majority of the tribes are inhabiting the hilly areas of Srikakulam, Vijayanagaram, Visakhapatnam, West Godavari, Khammam, Warangal, Medak and Adilabad districts. The remaining tribals are distributed in the plain areas of all the districts.

Among the tribes living in the plain areas of Andhra Pradesh, the Sugalis comprise one of the numerically dominant tribes. They are predominantly found in Anantapur, Chittoor, Guntur, Mahboobnagar, Krishna, Kurnool, Warangal and Adilabad districts of Andhra Pradesh. In Coastal Andhra and Rayalaseema region Sugalis are recognised as a Scheduled tribe, but in the Telangana region they are recognised as Denotified tribe.

According to the census of 1971, the Sugali population of Andhra Pradesh is 124,336 in a total population 43,502,708. In Chittoor district, with a population of 2,285,536, the Sugali population is 10,816. A majority of the Sugalis in Chittoor district are found in Madanapalli, Punganur and Chinnagottigallu taluks.

The Sugalis are known by different names such as Banjaras, Lambani, Brinjari, Vanjari, Boyapari, Sugali or Sukali in different regions of India. Pratap (1968) is of opinion that Sugali might have been a corruptive form of the Sanskrit word Sugwala (good cow-herd). But Ramachandra Reddy, M. (1984) report that some Sugalis from Sugalimitta and other villages of Chittoor district feel that the word 'Sugali' is derived from the word 'Supari' meaning 'Betelnut' (supari) since their ancestors once traded Supari.

Purpose of the Present Study

There is a dearth of scientific studies related to the child rearing practices of the tribes of Rayalaseema region. Hence the present study was undertaken to know the child rearing practices of Sugalimitta in Chittoor district which is in Rayalaseema area.

Soon after independence, the Government of India gave top priority to develop the nation in all sectors, as also to improve the living conditions of the Indian people. Various socio-economic welfare programmes and setting up of large scale and small scale industries were started to provide opportunities for people from all walks of life to participate and benefit from them. The scheduled tribals also had a chance to be exposed to various measures, after, some of them migrated from natural habitats to proximate industrial township. Consequently, it may be presumed that their traditional way of life were affected by the urban life style around them. This group which was influenced by the changed life style of the urban population are considered as the "transitional group" of tribals for the present study. Their life style is likely to be different from that of "Traditional group" which leads an isolated life in the hilly region. The present study is an attempt to know the differences in child rearing practices between the traditional and transitional Sugali tribals.

Objectives

The specific objectives are listed below:

1) To study the child rearing practices among traditional and transitional Sugalis and to make a comparison between the two;

2) To find out the effect of factors like economic status, education of the mother and age of the child on the child rearing practices among the traditional and transitional Sugalis.

Hypothesis

Based on the objectives the following major hypothesis was formed.

There are significant differences in the child rearing practices of the traditional and transitional Sugalis mainly in the specific areas like religious ceremonies performed on children, feeding practices, health and hygienic practices, disciplinary measures and parental educational aspirations for their children due to economic status, education of the mother and age of the child.

Based on the null hypothesis listed below, the data was analysed.

1) There are no significant differences in the performance of religious rituals for children by the traditional and transitional Sugalis.

2) There are no significant differences in the feeding practices of traditional and transitional Sugalis.

3) There are no significant differences in the health and hygienic practices of traditional and transitional Sugalis.

4) There are no significant differences in the disciplinary measures of traditional and transitional Sugalis.

6) There is no significant association between economic

status and child rearing practices of the Sugalis.

7) There is no significant association between education of the mother and child rearing practices of the Sugalis.

8) There is no significant association between age of the child and child rearing practices of the Sugalis.

2
Review of Literature

Many studies on child rearing practices have been undertaken. But studies on tribals are few and those on Sugali tribe are even fewer. Relevant studies have been reviewed and the findings have been reported under the following subtitles in a chronological order.

1. Practices related to marriage and child birth

2. Religious ceremonies performed on children

3. Feeding practices

4. Health and hygienic practices

5. Disciplinary measures

6. Parental educational aspirations for their children

Practices Related to Marriage and Child Birth

Marriage is an event of great social and religious significance and marks the first stage in the family-building process. Mahaboob Hussain, S.K. (1951) reported about marriage among the Koya tribe of Warangal, Karimnagar and Adilabad districts of Andhra Pradesh. Marriage within the gotra was prohibited among the Koyas, but marrying maternal uncle's daughter was permissible though marrying father's sister's daughter was rather rare.

Roy Burman, B.K. et al. (1961) reported about the age at marriage among the Lambadis of Andhra Pradesh. It ranged from 16-18 years for females and 18-25 years for males on an average.

Ahuja, R. (1966) analysed the marriage among the Bhil tribe of Rajasthan and found that 10 percent of the Bhils married before 15 years of age, 80.1 percent between 15 and 21 years of age and 2.0 percent after 24 years of age. Arranged marriages were common. Monogamy was the prevailing form of marriage. Bhils preferred to marry their children into families known to them directly or indirectly. In 60.96 percent cases, mates were selected from villages within 10 miles of one's own home.

Yadav, K.S. (1968) studied cross-cousin marriages among the Gonds living in the district of Chhindwara in Madhya Pradesh. An analysis of first marriages of 293 Gond males revealed at 59.04 percent were married to their cross-cousins (females). Among those who had married their cross-cousins, 73.41 percent were married to the mother's brother's daughter and 26.59 percent to their father's sister's daughter.

Vyas, N.N. (1970) reported about marriage among Bhils of Rajasthan. Generally Bhil girls were not married before puberty. Strict exogamy was noticed which prohibits girls to marry either within capture was prevalent among the Bhils.

Basu's, M.P. (1970) study revealed that inter and intra-village marriages were common among Banjaras of Himachal Pradesh. Female's marriage age ranged from 13 to 25 years, it was also found that all girls conceived during their marital life. None of them accepted birth control measures.

Das, R.K. (1972) reported about marriage and kinship among the Kabui Nagas of Manipur. They practiced matrilateral cross-cousin marriage which has a positive effect on their kinship system. Marriages of the type Fa Si So - Mo Br Da was customary while the other one Fa Si Da Mo Br So was absolutely prohibited.

Roychoudhary, A.K. (1976) pooled the state-wise consanguinity data for the tribals and obtained a value of 0.034 for Andhra Pradesh tribals. This rank was found to come next to Maharashtra and Kerala.

Mahanta, K.C. (1977) reported about marriage practices among Nocte tribe of Arunachal Pradesh. Normally for boys the age of marriage was 21-25 years and for girls 16-20 years. The notable feature of the Nocte marriage system was to develop marital alliance with persons with whom there was at least some degree of familiarity. Personal knowledge about a prospective mate was considered necessary in the event of marriage.

Narahari, S. (1982) noticed around 40-50 percent of consanguineous marriages among the Yerukulas of Andhra Pradesh.

Pandu Ranga Swamy, K. (1983) conducted a study on population structure of Sugalis of Kurnool district in Andhra Pradesh and found that the general marriage system was monogamy. Maternal cross-cousin marriages were preferred. Sugalis preferred early marriages and no male was found to be unmarried after 20 years of age. The basic unit in Sugalis was a nuclear family type.

Mukhopadhyay's R. (1984) study revealed that the age at marriage among Chenchus of Andhra Pradesh varied from 16 to 20 years in case of females and between 21 to 25 years in case of males. Marriage by negotiation was a common feature among them. Fifty percent of the families were of 'nuclear' type. The 'joint' or 'extended' families were minimum in number.

Sibajuddin, S.M. (1984) studied reproduction and consanguinity among Chenchus of Andhra Pradesh and found that the fertility ratio (71.83) was high even with reference to the other tribal populations of India. Due to the early marriage of both the sexes and non-adoption of family planning methods, the mean of live born children for each fertility completed mother was observed to be high. The consanguinity rate of the Chenchus was moderate, characterised by uncle-niece marriages.

Yaseen Saheb, S. and Ananda Bhanu, B. (1984) reported about consanguinity among the Irular of Tamilnadu. The consanguinity rate was higher among the isolated group (51.09%) than in the exposed group (38.71%) with an average of 43.98 percent. The first cross cousin marriages were commonly seen with marrying maternal uncle's daughters in isolated (22.83%) and exposed (12.90%) groups. The uncle niece marriages were only 10-19 percent among the Irular, with a higher proportion among the exposed group (11.29%) than among isolated group (8.70%).

Rohini, A. and Reddi, G.G. (1985) studied some demographic trends among the tribal women of Andhra Pradesh and found that the marriages of Bagathas, Valmiki and Savara tribals were performed mostly at the age of 15-17 years. But among Bagathas, the child marriages were seen frequently. In all the three groups, the highest incidence of first conception was found in the age of 15-19 years.

Narahari's, S. (1985) study reported about Nakkala tribe of Southern India. They were found to prefer and practice consanguineous marriages. Both types of cross cousin marriages, matrilateral (Mo Br Da) and patrilateral (Fa Si Da) were seen frequently.

Naik, S. and Sharma, A.K. (1985) study revealed that the age at marriage among Bhuiyan tribal women was 13-16 years, while for men 15-18 years. As the couple had no knowledge of family planning, fertility was generally high. It had been observed that money was the main incentive for adopting sterilization.

Majumdar, B. (1986) reported about marriage practices of Totos tribe in Bengal. Marriage was not allowed within the same clan. Cross-cousin marriage was the general custom.

Singh, R. (1987) reported about marriage and law among Bhils of Rajasthan. Arranged marriages were the most common pattern among them. When a boy attained the age of 16 years or so the parents and other relatives of the family were found to search for a suitable girl within the community. Clan exogamy was strictly observed and mother's clan was also avoided while selecting a girl.

Practices related to child birth among tribals also studied by many researchers, Sarker, A. Choudhuri, N. and Sankar Ray, G. (1955) reported about birth and pregnancy rites among the Oraon tribe of Bihar. Among Oraons, pregnancy taboos with regard to sex, food and movement were observed. Cohabitation was not permissible after four months of pregnancy. They were restricted from eating meet, edible herbs. After the third month of pregnancy, a women were avoided from doing heavy domestic work and not allowed to go to the cremation ground.

Nag's, M.K. (1954) survey revealed that the prevalence of higher percentage of nuclear families among Lambadis and Chenchus of Andhra Pradesh, Soligaru of Karnataka and Kanikkar of Kerala.

Swaroop, R. (1963) stated that among certain primitive tribes the cravings of an expectant mother are regarded as sacred wishes, which must be fulfilled.

Sinha, R.K. (1977) studied about family composition among the Pando tribe of Madhya Pradesh and found ordinarily, that nuclear type of family was popular among them. Although, extended and composite type of families were witnessed but they were less popular.

Sinha, R.K. (1984) reported about pregnancy taboos of Bhilala tribe of Madhya Pradesh, Gujarat and Rajasthan. The taboos were crossing a broom-stick and the tying ropes of horse, ass and mare. They had a belief that the above said animals deliver their babies only in twelve months. Thus, a violation of the above taboo may lead to the same consequence to a pregnant women and deliver a baby in the 12th month. Another taboo also observed that was seeing a dead body.

Gurumurthy, G. (1984) study revealed that 85 percent of the Yanadis of Chittoor district, Andhra Pradesh, believed that the child birth is the grace and gift of God, it is the destiny to have the large number of children. Seventy percent of Yanadis felt that 'son is a must' over one-third (36%) had the belief that God might punish them if they adopt family planning which is a sin.

Some of the researchers studied about the practices related to marriage and child birth among the non-tribals. Minturn, L. and Hitchcock, J.T. (1964) conducted a study on Rajputs of Khalapur and found that the girls were generally married at 16 or 17 years and boys at 18 or 20 years. Taboos during pregnancy were observed and they included the avoiding of milk, cold rice, a pulse dish, food which is either excessively 'hot' or excessively 'cold' and spicy foods such as pickles. Devadas, R.P. (1968) reported that in some South Indian villages, no special food was given to pregnant women, but the quantity of rice and milk were restricted from fear of the foetus becoming 'big' and making the delivery difficult. The lactating mother was given extra milk, ghee, garlic rasam and jaggery water for increasing breast milk. Lahiri, S. (1970) findings in urban India showed a very great preference for sons in all sectors of population. The reasons for preference of sons expressed by them were as follows: 1) they are responsible for the perpetuation of the family name; 2) sons take the responsibility of looking after parents in old age; 3) parents feel that sons are a great asset to help in their work; 4) son should perform all religious rites like the lighting the funeral pyre and performing death ceremonies. He also reported that generally 3 or 4 children were considered ideal by a large proportion of population.

Basu, S.K. (1977) studied the effects of consanguinity among Muslims and found that high parental consanguinity both among Sayyad and Shaik (49.40%) of Lucknow and Darvoodi Bohras (41.79%) of Udaipur. Puri, R.K., Verma, I.C. and Bhargava, I. (1978) studied the effects of consanguinity among the people of Pondicherry showed 55.1 percent were of consanguineous and 44.9 percent were of non-consanguineous with highest frequency in Muslims (72.2%) followed by Brahmins (67.0%). A higher frequency of consanguineous marriages were noted among the illiterates. Mainzen, R.S. (1980) study revealed about norms and realities of marriage arrangements in a South Indian town. For the present generation, the average age of boys at the time of marriage was 28.7 years and for girls 23.0 years. This rise in marriage age is largely due to education. Reddy's, P.C. (1983) study reported the frequency of first cross cousin marriages were common among the Malas of Chittoor district, Andhra Pradesh. Devadas, R.P. and Easwaran, P.P. (1986) conducted a study on food consumption pattern of pregnant mothers of the rural areas of Madhurai namely Oddenchatram. The foods like papaya and drumstick leaves were tabooed for the fear of causing abortion and indigestion respectively. The pregnant mother did not receive any priority in food intake.

Religious Ceremonies Performed on Children

According to the Grihasutras every stage in the life of an individual is marked by some sort of rituals. Tribals perform their birth-rites and rituals associated with their various beliefs and practices.

Dube, L. (1949) reported about pregnancy and child birth among the Amat Gonds, Raipur district and stated that the Chhatti (purificatory) and name-giving ceremony were performed on the sixth day after delivery. Birth of the first child and specially that of the first male child was celebrated with great enthusiasm.

Mahboob Hussain, S.K. (1951) reported about the Koya tribe which is generally found in Warangal, Karimnagar and Adilabad districts of Andhra Pradesh. Among the Koyas it was customary that to perform Chatti on the third day after delivery and the name giving ceremony on the fifth day. Generally the names of deceased family members were given.

Sarker, A., Choudhari, N. and Sankar Ray, G. (1955) collected case histories among the Oraons of Chaha village in the district of Ranchi, Bihar Sate. They found that on the sixth day after delivery the Chhatti ceremony was performed. On that day the whole family mother, child and all the members in the family had a purificatory bath.

Mundri, L.S. (1956) conducted a study on birth ceremonies among Munda tribe which is located in village Katowa, Ranchi district at Bihar and found that a period of ceremonial impurity was observed by the family for seven days. It commenced on the date of the child-birth and ended when the purification ceremony called Chhatti was performed. No villager enters the house during this impurity period and vice-versa. If any one entered the house by mistake he or she can enter his or her house only after taking a ceremonial bath after anointing their body with Karanj oil mixed with turmeric. Name-giving ceremony was performed on Chhatti day itself. Mostly they select some of the ancestor's names for children.

Jha, M. (1963) studied the Ollar who are mainly concentrated in Koraput district of Orissa and found that Name-giving ceremony was performed after about 2 weeks of the birth of a child. The name was given according to the days of the week on which the baby was born. Sometimes the names were given as per the instructions of the Disari (Priest).

Bahadur, K.P. (1977) reported about the purificatory ceremony among the Banjaras of Andhra Pradesh, when a child was born. The period of impurity for the mother was reckoned as five days. On the sixth day the purificatory ceremony was performed by washing the feet of all the children of the hamlet and giving them food to eat.

Sinha, R.K. (1984) observed birth-rites and rituals among the Bhilala tribe of Madhya Pradesh, Gujarat and Rajasthan. He observed that besides purificatory and tonsure ceremony, they offered one full coconut on the birth of male child and half-a-coconut on the birth of female child, in the bon-fire on the Holi. Again on the second day of the Holi, the head of the family out off a little hair of the new-born and buried it with one piece of bread.

From the above studies it is seen that the Koyas of Andhra Pradesh, Oraons of Bihar, Mundas of Bihar, Ollar of Orissa, Banjaras of Andhra Pradesh, Bhilalas of Madhya Pradesh perform Chhatti and name-giving ceremonies.

The purificatory and name-giving ceremonies were found to be a common practice among other communities in India. Minturn, L. and Hitchcock, J.T. (1964) reported that Rajputs of Khalapur performed specific ceremonies namely Bahari, Jasutan in connection with the male child's birth in addition to the Chotili (purificatory) and Mundan hair-cutting ceremonies. Aphale's, C. (1976) study in Poona revealed that the Chaula or tonsure ceremony was performed by a majority of Scheduled Caste families and that the naming ceremony of girls was not celebrated as that of boys. Reddy, A.B. and Reddy, S.B. (1977), Saibaba, K. Reddy, S.V.B. and Reddy, S.P. (1979) carried out some studies on life cycle ceremonies in lower classes in different parts of Andhra Pradesh, and noticed that all of them performed naming and cradling ceremonies in association with each other though the age at which these ceremonies were performed were found to be different in different communities. They noticed that the tonsure ceremony was performed as per their convenience either at the 1st year, 3rd year, or 5th year after delivery. Usha Rani, K. (1980) studied the life cycle ceremonies of males in Chittoor district and found that on the day of purification (11th day) the child was put in a cradle and was given a name. This study also revealed that they performed tonsure ceremony in the 11th month or after an age of 3 years or during on any odd year of the child. Mukhopadhyay, R. (1984) reported about child birth among the Chenchus of Andhra Pradesh. The purificatory and name giving ceremonies were performed on the 21st day after child birth. Prathusha, S.K. (1985) study reported that namakaranam and cradling ceremony was carried out on the day of 'purudu' (purificatory) or 11th day after birth by the Harijans of Chittoor district. Name was given to the child by looking at the horoscope and birth star. Tonsure ceremony was conducted in the 9th or 11th month or in the 3rd or 5th year after birth on an auspicious day.

Feeding Practices

There are cultural attitudes, values, practices and beliefs regarding the intake of food among different groups in a community. Dube, L. (1949) report about pregnancy and child birth practices among the Amat Gonds of Raipur district, observed that feeding was continued as long as the mother had milk. If the mother conceives again, she allow the child to suck till the foetus is about five months old or till the pregnancy is confirmed. For making it forget mother's milk a child was given such alluring things as roti, chana, murra (fried rice) or tea. But if it persisted in not giving up it's right, a bitter paste of neem leaves was applied to the breasts of the mother, with that reason child got an aversion for sucking.

Belavady, B. et al. (1959) conducted studies on lactation and dietary habits of the tribes of Nilgiri in Tamil Nadu. The results indicated that the majority of tribal women breast-fed their infants for periods upto two or three years. Though supplements were started invariably in the earlier half of the first year, the impression of the authors was that these supplements were of a poor quality.

Sampath, R. (1964) studied the child care and child-rearing practices among the Gonds of Tamia and found that their children were breast fed until they could walk and take food by their own hand.

Bahl, L. (1979) reported about infant feeding practices among the tribals of Himachal Pradesh. The results showed that 84 percent of the children were given their first feed 12 hours after birth. Most mothers breast fed their children upto 36 months. At the age of 13-24 months 92 percent of children received semisolid foods. Meat, eggs and milk were considered nutritious foods and so were given to the children.

Mudgal, S. and Rajput, V.S. (1979) conducted a survey on infant feeding practices of tribals of Madhya Pradesh. Most of them believed that breast feeding should start within 6 hrs. of birth and that it should be prolonged. Colostrum was not discarded. Semisolid food was introduced within 6 months, but only cereal was given. Nearly 2/3rd of women believed that food should not be restricted for a sick child.

Narayan, S. (1983) studied the health care of the Oraon children from the Barambe village in Ranchi district, Bihar and found that the Oraon child totally depended on mother's milk till the age of one year. After the completion of a year the baby was given solid food.

Dave, P., Hakim, M. and Tavkar, N. (1984) undertook a research project in Panchamahal district, Gujarat to study the child care amongst the tribals. Regarding the feeding practices, they observed that breast feeding on demand was the rule. The frequency of breast feeding the child decreased with increase in age. This study also revealed that weaning was begun after the child starts walking. A majority of the children were completely weaned between the age of

2 to 2½ years. This study showed no significant sex differences as far as the age of weaning starting and completing.

Swain, L. (1985) studied the infant feeding practices among Santal tribe in northern orissa and found that immediately after the child's birth, honey or jaggery - which they believe, could help the child resist hunger - was given to the child. The child was usually put to breast after 12 hrs. Breast feeding was encouraged in the children till the mother conceives again. The supplementary feeding to the baby started when the child reached the age of seven months. They used soft rice, gruel and pulses as a major supplementary food.

Dave, C. (1985) studied infant feeding practices in tribal pockets of Udaipur district, Rajasthan and found that 57 percent of mothers were breast feeding the infant till the child reached two years of age. regarding weaning practices, the majority of the mothers started weaning their children from the age of one year.

The A.P.A.U. report (1983) of profile of tribal families in East Godavari district revealed that breast feeding to the neonate was started on the first day of delivery in majority of the cases or as soon as milk-letting occurred. Until breast feeds were initiated, the neonate was not given anything. Breast feeding was continued upto 2 years in 40 percent of the cases. 25 percent of children were fed on breast milk without any supplementary food till three years of age. Children hardly received any supplementary food as long as they were breast fed.

The report of Vimala, V. and Ratnaprabha, C. (unpublished) on infant feeding practices prevalent among tribal communities of Bhadragiri, Vizianagaram district, Andhra Pradesh. From that investigation certain good practices have been observed among tribal mothers. Early breast feeding (95%) and acceptance of colostrum (100%) were the beneficial practices observed in the community. In case of lactation failure, the child was fed on cow's milk or gruels of cereals and millets. Breast feeding was continued till next pregnancy or till cessation of milk.

Das, K. and Ghosh, A.K. (1985) found that breast feeding was the main form of food for the infants among the Santhals of Bihar. They believed that breast milk of sick mother is harmful for the health of the baby. In such cases cow's milk was preferred as replacement and the same was introduced though they regarded cow' milk to be too heavy and causing indigestion or stomach disorder to the babies. There was a common belief that if the calf is deprived of its mothers' (cow's) milk then the baby's mother would not yield any milk. Goat's milk was avoided as they believe that the babies became restless and troublesome after consuming it. Normally, the child was breast fed for a long time until a subsequent one is born. The introduction of solid food was started in regular manner only around one to one and half years of age or even later. Now-a-days, some of the mothers are introducing 'canned baby food' due to higher income level.

Rizvi, S.N.H. (1985) conducted a study on the Jaunsaris of Uttar Pradesh and found that the neonates and infants were usually suckled by the mother and that breast feeding usually continued upto the age of 2 or 3 years or till the delivery of the next child, whichever was earlier. The infants started eating cereals at the age of six to seven months or at the most eight months, while they still continue to be breast fed. The semi-solid foods which were given to the child in the initial phase were 'Kangni' which was prepared with rice cooked in surplus water to make it dilute. Bread was also started at this age.

From the above studies it is found that most tribal groups have ideal practices like feeding the new born with colostrum, prolonged breast feeding.

Some of the recent non-tribal studies in the area of feeding practices are summarised. Bailure, A. (1971) studied food consumption patterns of pre-school children in six cities of India, and found that breast feeding was a universal practice and continued upto two or even three years, pregnancy was major reason for stoppage. Supplementations started by 2 years and weaning was completed by 4 or 5 years. Madhavi, V. Rao, P.N. and Mathew, Y.C. (1972) study in the village Fatehpur, Hyderabad, revealed that infants were fed on breast after 36 to 48 hours of birth and prolonged breast feeding was common. Bhandari, N.R. and Patel, G.P. (1973) study reported that the mothers of all socio-economic groups in Bhopal, Madhya Pradesh, accepted breast feeding as natural and new born were put to breast between one to six days. Solids were introduced mostly at one year and mainly consisted of carbohydrates. Walia, B.N.S. et al (1974) study in an urban population of Chandigarh indicated that the act of weaning was highly correlated with socio-economic status. 75 percent of upper class made an attempt to wean the babies by about nine months. 70.7 percent of all mothers continued breast feeding beyond

12 months. Datta Banik, N.D. (1975) study in Delhi revealed that majority of infants were put on breast by 13-24 hours after delivery. 97.3 percent children were either completely or partially breast-fed upto 6 months, 55.8 percent till age of 1½ years and 2.1 percent to age of 4 years. Most mothers of higher socio-economic group started solid food at about 6 months, while mothers of lower socio-economic group started it after one year. Puri, R.K. et al (1976) studied the infant feeding and child rearing methods followed in Pondicherry and found that Sugar water was the initial prelacteal feed in a majority of cases. In about 50 percent of cases, breast feeding was delayed beyond the first 48 hrs. of life and breast feeding was found to be universal. A study on infant feeding practices in rural and urban areas in Madhya Pradesh was carried out by Patodi, R.K. et al (1976) and found that 50 percent of urban and 80 percent of rural mothers gave breast milk to their infants. It was observed that the most common age of weaning was 13 to 15 months in the rural area, while in urban areas it was 10 to 12 months. Saraswathi's, S. (1978) study in rural Orissa revealed that the child for the first few days was fed on pure honey and on 3rd day it was put on the mother's breast. Breast feeding was encouraged in the children till the mother conceives again. Weaning was initiated in majority of cases in the sixth month. Bhogie, S. (1978) studied the child rearing practices among three cultures namely caste Hindus, Backward Hindus, Muslims in Hyderabad and found that the majority of the caste Hindus and backward Hindus started breast feeding on the third day and Muslim mothers started it on the fifth day. Muslim mothers were found to prefer either bottle or breast feeding while most of the backward Hindu mothers breast fed their children. Almost all of them considered the seventh month to be the most auspicious time to introduce solid food. In Haryana, Kaur, M., Sisodia, G.S. and Mehra, S. (1979) found that in 38 percent of cases brandy was the first oral feed given after delivery. Mother's milk was given to the child only on the 3rd day and from that time onwards all of them breast fed their children. The mean age upto which a child was breast fed was 30.9 months. According to Kakar, S. (1979) an Indian mother is inclined towards a total indulgence of her infant's wishes and demands. Feeding is frequent at all times of the day and night and on demand. Although breast feeding is supplemented with other kind of food after the first year, the mother continues to give her breast to the child for as long as possible-often upto two or three years. Rajalakshmi's, M. (1979) study in Karnataka revealed that the women in the village

nearer to urban centres stopped breast feeding after the child was one year old. But women who lived in remote areas, further away from the urban centres, continued to breast feed their children until the subsequent pregnancy forces them to stop. Regarding weaning, women in the more remote village introduced solid foods earlier though they breast fed longer. Nirmala, K. et al's (1981) study in Devangere, revealed that breast-feeding upto one year was observed in 86 percent of cases and upto two years of age in 48 percent of cases irrespective of whether the mother belonged to rural and urban area. For only 10 percent of children, weaning was started before the age of 3 months. Semisolids were introduced for about half the children between 6 to 12 months. By 18 months 42 percent of the children were getting semisolids. Indira Bai, K. et al's (1981) study in Tirupati reported that breast feeding was more common in rural areas than in the urban areas. In the rural area most children were weaned on to solids without intervening supplementary feeds with fresh or artificial milk.

Health and Hygienic Practices

Health problems and health practices of any community are profoundly influenced by the interplay of a complex of social, economic and political factors. These factors have also had considerable influence not only on the development of medical technology but also in determining the access of different social strata of a community to such technology.

As far as the tribal communities are concerned, they have their own cultural identity and as its component a health culture.

Roy, S.C. and Majumdar, D.N. (1933) reported about tribal health and medicine in the ethnographic studies made on tribal communities. It indicated that a number of deities are often associate with diseases or disease and that the nature of treatment in such cases is also associated with the influence of supernatural agency.

Elwin, V. (1953) had shown a great interest in tribal health and medicine and made a number of studies on tribal communities. He indicated the importance of understanding the socio-cultural dimensions of health and disease.

Narayan, S. (1983) studied the health care of the Oraon children of Barambe village in Ranchi district, Bihar and found that children usually did not clean their teeth upto the age of eight. They hardly had bath once in fortnight. Only 30 percent of them had some kind of cloth to wear on the upperpart of the body and to cover their private parts. It was only after the age of five that clothes were considered essential for them and one set of dress was provided. The parents were not aware of small-pox vaccination or immunization for polio, diptheria and tetanus etc. Malaria, cholera, dysentery, throat infections and diarrhoeas were common diseases of the village during hot as well as rainy seasons and fever was common in the children of oraon for which they hardly administered any medicine unless it become serious. Children usually used the areas around the house for toilet purposes.

Profile of tribal families in East Godavari district reported by APAU (1983) that fever, respiratory, infection, gestroenteritis and scabies were most common ailments in children. The treatment practices adopted by the tribals observed that about 40-50 percent of them were going for allopathy treatment for common diseases. Even the other 50 percent who were not going for allopathy might be due to inaccessibility of health centre rather than their disapproval. Out of this 50 percent, a considerable number had not taken any treatment especially for fever and respiratory infections. A significant number depended on the local men who give herbal medicines for common illness. They tried to have some indigenous medicine for diarrhoeas which may or may not be effective in controlling.

Dave, P., Hakim, M, and Tavkar, N. (1984) studied child care amongst the tribals of Gujarat and found that there was no particular age at which the mothers toilet trained the child. The mothers were not particular about training the children, for achieving independence at an earlier age. Till 4 years of age the child generally moved around in an upper garment or nothing at all, so the question of changing the soiled clothes seldom arose. The child was bathed with warm water. Bathing the child was the mother's job till the baby reach 5 years of age. The child's physical care was neglected. The child was unkempt and was shabbily and meagerly dressed. The common cold was a very common ailment but no special attention was given to the child suffering from cold. The treatment for sick children was usually availed from the village Bhagat. The magico religious belief in evil spirits evidently have a stronger hold as it out-numbers hygienic considerations. Sorcery was linked with causing and curing diseases. As a result of such faith in the supernatural, the tribals availed of the alien allopathic services only when local resources were exhausted.

Chowdhuri, M.K., De, S. and Debnath, A. (1985) conducted a survey on impact of prevalent diseases among the tribals of tribal concentrated areas of West Bengal and found that the tribal people were quite ignorant of many of the diseases. The knowledge in health and hygiene and preventive measures were more or less absent. The village medicine-men generally treated and prescribed for most of the diseases prevalent in the area, excepting the leprosy. The benefit of modern treatment is yet to be accepted by the tribal communities as they still hold their traditional cultural beliefs and practices.

Dash, J. (1985) reported about the concept and treatment of disease by Paraja tribe of Orissa. In the Paraja social system, the concept and treatment of the diseases were found to be very much associated with the magico-religious beliefs. Most of the diseases were believed to be caused due to the wrath of the deities, spirit intrusion, casting of evil eye and breach of social-cultural norms. The herbal medicines also occupied a very important position in their indigenous methods of treatment.

Das, K. and Ghosh, A.K. (1985) conducted a study on the Santhals of Bihar to observe the health care of their children and it revealed that if children are significantly ill and do not immediately respond to domestic medicine or medicine given by the folk practitioners (ojha) then only they take the patients to modern doctors.

Some of the researchers conducted studies among non-tribals also to know their health and hygienic practices. Dube, S.C. (1958) studied the health and hygienic practices in villages in Uttar Pradesh as a part of the work of National community Development Programme. The survey revealed that the villages on the whole were insanitary and health and hygienic practices were not good. Minturn, L, and Hitchcock's, J.T. (1964) study also reported that many children contracted malaria and sore eyes repeatedly, small-pox or chicken pox, measles, boils, colds, pneumonia were common ailments for children and treatment given was herb medicines, massage, prayers and offerings as well as treatment by people skilled in magic, such as wandering holymen, or by sadhus and sianas. Gosh's B.N. (1966) study in Pondicherry, South India and the findings indicated that poor standards of hygiene are cause for malnourishment in younger children. Coffee was introduced as a preventive against coughs and colds. Bhogle, S. (1978) study also reported that the majority of the caste

Hindus and Backward Hindus bathed the child everyday. Muslim mothers believed that not bathing the child every day prevents colds. There were also differences with regard to the material used to bathe the baby. It included items like oil, soap, milk, flour and haldi. Both caste Hindu mothers and Backward Hindu mothers believed that the use of these items strengthened and smoothened the baby's body, while Muslim mothers did not give any definite reason.

Pandey, D.N., Agnihotri, S.N. and Srivastave, A.K. (1979) reported that 22.2 percent of children had been immunized against such diseases as tetanus and small-pox. Immunization in the males and in the eldest children was higher than in female and younger children. Immunization was more common in children belonging to middle-income families and in children whose mothers were literates. Kaur, M., Sisodia, G.S. and Mehra, S. (1979) reported regarding personal hygiene that bathing and changing clothes of the child was observed to be less in the lower castes. They further found that diseases like fever, cold, cough, diarrhoes, dysentery, whooping cough, constipation were highly prevalent and that home treatment was used for their cure in children. The toilet training of the child was found to be very casual, especially in the lower class. Madhavi, J. (1979) and Hemalatha Rani, P. (1980) found that the children in villages of Chittoor district, were usually given bath twice or thrice in a week and most of them were seen naked. To cure cold, mothers used the juice of occimum basilicus (Kukkathulasi) and for whooping cough, the fruits of Kanuga (Pongamiaglabra) were tied around the neck of the child. Only a few villagers availed of the medical services available. Sobhavathi, J. (1980) reported about the Harijans of Charala village in Chittoor district and found that the personal hygienic habits were not good. Many children were found to suffer from minor ailments like fever, cold and cough. The treatment given to children comprised of folk medicines, magical treatment. In a few cases however allopathic medicines were used in case of emergencies. Nagabhushanamma, K. (1984) studied Harijans in Chittoor district and found that majority of the children among the salaried group were getting daily bath which was not the case with those in the daily wage group. Regarding the frequency of changing clothes it was noticed that 62 percent of parents in the farmer group were changing their children's clothes daily and the corresponding ration among daily wage group was only 30 percent. She further noticed that the belief in magical and indigenous treatment was very strong and that only a few availed the medical services.

Disciplinary Measures

Discipline has double function of taking care of the present situation and at the same time preparing for the future. The pre-school period is the time for the parent to establish the basic principles of the plan of discipline.

The studies on disciplinary measures among tribals are very few. Some studies on non-tribal communities in India and other countries undertaken and presented in detail.

Radke, M.J. (1946) studied 43 children of nursery school or kindergarten age, giving the parents a questionnaire and observing the children in free play and picture interpretation test situations. Children from more restrictive and autocratic home discipline showed less aggressiveness, less rivalry, were more passive, more colorless and were less popular. They did not get-along so well with other children. The children from homes with free discipline were more active, showed more rivalry and were more popular.

Ayer, M.E. and Berneuter, R.A. (1951) reported on an other study of the personality traits of nursery school children in relation to their home discipline. Significant correlations appeared between physical punishment at home and a tendency of children not to face reality and between permissiveness of parents (letting children learn from the natural consequences of their acts) and a more "attractive" personality in the child.

Sears, R., Maccoby, E. and Levin, H. (1957) studied the child rearing practices of 379 mothers of five-year old children. The socio-economic status of these mothers as classified by the investigators as either 'middle class' or 'working class'. They found that middle class mothers imposed fewer restrictions on their children and made fewer demands upon them than did the working class mothers. In general the middle class mothers were less punitive and more permissive towards their children than were the lower class mothers.

Ames, E. and Randeri, K. (1965) conducted a study to observe some differences in child rearing practices of Indian and Canadian mothers. Canadian and Indian mothers of children matched for sex, age, religion and language were interviewed. It was found that

Canadians employ spanking or beating where as Indians used rejection methods for punishment. There were no differences in the use of scolding or withholding of privileges as a form of punishment. Canadian mothers more often practice early training of the child and then refuse to help him with what he is supposed to know, while Indian mothers let the child solve problems for himself, but are more willing to help him.

The influence of socio-economic status of family on various aspects of parent-child interaction has been studied by a number of research workers. Kohn, H.L. and Carroll, E.E. (1966) examined the different types of disciplinary methods preferred by members of different social class. They found that middle class parents regard it as of primary importance that a child be able to decide for himself how to act on his decisions. To working class parents however it is important that a child acts reputably and without breaking rules.

Muthayya's, B.C. (1972) study near Hyderabad, Andhra Pradesh revealed that the majority of the parents mentioned that they would spank the child. The next higher percentage respondents indicated that the child would be given advice. Punishment was severe by mothers when compared with the fathers. The punishment accorded was lenient in the high socio-economic status group compared with low socio-economic status group.

Sidana, U. R.and Sinha, D. (1973) conducted a study in Kanpur city aimed to find out the relationship between the child rearing practices of the parents and the development of fears in children and found that children who were less often punished by their parents had fewer fears than those who were more often punished.

Aphale's, C. (1976) study also revealed that the parents were little aware of the probable ill-effects of their threatening or beating children and used these measures frequently. Children were disciplined by parents in a haphazard manner and no care was taken to see that children observed the prescribed norms.

A study on the child rearing in a Colombian village was made by Reichel, A.D. (1979). Here the severity of the punishment was found to be dependent on the mothers up-bringing and the poorest mothers seemed to punish their children most severely. Much stress is laid on the importance of avoiding physical punishment, for fear that too much of it will make the child become a person without shame.

Ideally it is said that child should be so well brought up that it can be controlled with a glance. Another method of punishment is to frighten children by putting them in a dark place.

Singh, M.B. and Kaur, S. (1981) studied mother-child interaction in rural and urban areas of India. Results shown that rural mothers interacted more with girls than with boys. They felt that girls needed more instruction and discipline than did boys. Mother-child interaction was greater when mothers had more education. Both urban and rural mothers used tactics such as attention diversion, discouragement, scolding and spanking to discipline their children.

Sharma, V.P. (1981) conducted a study on child rearing practices and child growth in an Indian urban families, Ahmedabad and found that the highly educated mothers tended to use reasoning, persuasion and reproach, more of the less educated mothers used spanking (such methods as 'calling names' or uttering futile threats or spanking are more in the interest of giving mother an immediate relief.

Grantham-McGregor, S., Landman, J. and Desai, P. (1982) studied the child rearing practices in poor urban Jamaica and found that most mothers (59 out of 75) beat their children with an implement, usually a belt or stick.

Nagabhushanamma, K. (1984) reported about disciplinary methods used by parents in Harijan community that a larger proportion of the parents who were daily wage earners tended to use physical punishment as compared to those with regular income. Physical punishment tended to be used more often by parents in large families as against those with fewer children.

Parental Educational Aspirations for their Children

Very few studies on tribal communities deal with parental educational aspirations for their children, Mandal, P.K. (1977) reported on the Santhals of Kapileswar, West Bengal. The Santhals were mostly illiterates. He found that they did not feel the necessity of education was for the "Babus" (high Caste Hindus).

Joshi, D.C. (1982) studied educational problems of the Scheduled castes and Scheduled tribes of Baroda district and found that the parents of the Scheduled caste and Scheduled tribe students had a positive attitude towards education but were doubtful about the capabilities of their children. They complained about their inability to take interest in the day-to-day home work given by school for their children because of their own limitation. Thus the positive attitude become ineffective in bringing about the expected results.

Some studies on non-tribal communities as the one undertaken by Muthayya, B.C. (1972) report the aspiration of the parents for the education of their sons and daughters. A higher percentage of fathers (59.3%) and mothers (55.2%) in high socio-economic status group aspired for college/technical education for their sons whereas a higher percentage of fathers (45.8%) and mothers (38.2%) in the middle socio-economic status group aspired for higher secondary education for their sons and in low socio-economic group, a higher percentage of them thought that education was not necessary for their sons when compared with other groups. From high to low socio-economic status groups, the percentage of father and mother respondents who aspired for higher secondary education for girls was in the decreasing order. In the high socio-economic status group, a higher percentage of mothers (36.7%) aspired for higher secondary education for girls than the fathers (30.7%). But in the case of the respondents who mentioned that education was not necessary for girls, the percentages were in the decreasing order from low to high socio-economic status groups. In the low socio-economic status group, 45.2 percent of fathers and 59.5 percent of mothers mentioned that education was not necessary for girls.

Grover, S. (1977) studied parental aspirations as related to personality and school achievements of children in Chandigarh, Punjab State and found that there was a very high and significant correlation between father's and mother's aspirations for their sons. There was a positive and significant correlation between parent's aspirations and the self-concept of their sons. High aspirations of parents led to low dominance in sons. The school achievements of sons of low aspiration parents were better than the sons of average aspiring parents and high aspiring parents.

Kaur, M., Sisodia, G.S., Mehra, S. (1979) found that in a majority (72%) of cases children in Haryana were not helped in learning to read. The majority of respondents thought that either there was no need for educating the child or that the child was very small. Literacy of the mother was positively associated with helping the child in learning to read.

Sharma, V.P. (1981) conducted a study on child earning practices and child growth in an Indian urban families, Ahmedabad and reported that 60 percent of mothers thought it 'very important' that children do well in school, i.e., 'School achievement' (working women are a bit more eager). Most of the mothers mentioned 'precise vocational targets' and firm aspirations for their children. The aspirations are mostly 'doctor, engineer and scientist'. One-third of the mothers cherish aspirations dependent on child's abilities and inclinations. However mother of 'only child' tends to expect that her child would fulfil parent's expectations. Nine out of ten mothers who had only one child expected their children to do so.

3
Methodology

Area of the Study

The investigator decided to conduct a study on Sugalis of Chittoor district, Andhra Pradesh. As Chittoor district is a hilly area, the Sugalis are found in this area. The investigator selected 'Sugalimitta' area which is located in Punganur Mandal, Chittoor district, about 10 Kms. away from the taluk headquarters. The different criteria governing the selection of this Sugalimitta thandas are as follows:

1) The Sugalis residing in Sugalimitta is a representative sample of the group in Chittoor district.

2) It's closeness to Tirupati from where the investigator had to carry out the research.

3) Convenience in reaching

Sugalis have three subgroups namely 1) Bhukia 2) Mude and 3) Bhanavathi. These are exogamous units and are equated to clans. Sugalis generally live in clusters known as Thandas. The Sugalis of Sugalimitta live in seven detached clusters (thandas). Among the seven thandas, the investigator selected three—Peddathanda, Nallaguttapalli thanda and Chinna thanda for present study.

The chief characteristics of Sugalis of Peddathanda, Nallaguttapalli thanda regions are given below:

1. Residence :   They generally stay in the hill or in the forest region in the inaccessible parts. Hence they are not much exposed to the civilized world.

2. Occupation : Besides agriculture, their chief occupation is collecting and selling the firewood and forest produce. They are inclined to cattle rearing as well. Some of them are hunters.

3. Income :   Most of the members of the group are economically very poor with the annual income less than Rs. 2000/- Thus it is found that all of them are found to live below the poverty line.*

4. Language :   Their main dialect spoken by the Sugalis of the region is an admixture of Punjabi and Gujarathi. But many of them can speak Telugu.

5. Food habits : Their staple food is a coarse cake made of jowar or wheat. Some of them occasionally use rice. They are largely non-vegetarians. During festive occasions they prepare sweet with rice flour and jaggery. A few of them drink coffee or tea occasionally. They are fond of strong liquor. Both males and females chew pans.

6. Dress pattern : The women wear a very peculiar skirt of coarse red cotton cloth, embroidered on the border. Some small round mirror pieces are fixed all over the skirt. They wear blouses which is open at the back and is rich in embroidery work. They invariably cover their heads with another coloured piece of cloth. The men wear coloured or white handloom shirts and dhotis. They wear turban on their heads.

7. Ornaments: All females have numerous ornaments and include string of glass and beads besides those of brass and other metals. The married women have bangles of horns up to shoulders whereas unmarried up to elbow. They use different types of

---

* Poverty line is annual household income of Rs. 6,400/- in rural areas and Rs. 7,300/- in the urban areas.

anklets and toe rings. Some men wear only finger and toe rings of silver.

Sugalis of Chinnathanda differ from those staying at Peddathanda and Nallaguttapalli thanda. They have certain features in the following respects.

1. Residence: The houses of Sugalis are situated along main road side. Hence they are getting expose to the civilized world.

2. Occupation :   Majority of them are employees in Government institutions. Agriculture, collection of minor forest products, selling of fire-wood are some of the secondary sources of income.

3. Income :   Though their annual income is below the poverty line, most of the people are found to have annual income Rs. 2000/- to 4000/-.

4. Language :   They speak Telugu fluently apart from their tribal dialect.

5. Food habits :   Their diet consists of rice and curries etc. Some of them are interested in liquor.

6. Dress pattern :   The women wear sarees and blouses. Men wear pants and shirts.

7. Ornaments :   The women wear simple ornaments like neck chain, bangles, ear and nose rings, etc.

Sample of the Study

The characteristics of the Sugalis of Peddathanda and Nallaguttapalli thanda are similar to the characteristics of traditional tribal groups. On the other hand the Sugalis of Chinnathanda are in transitional stage. The investigator selected traditional type of Peddathanda and Nallaguttapalli thanda to study the child rearing practices among traditional Sugalis. The investigator also selected transitional type of Chinnathanda to study the child rearing practices among transitional Sugalis.

Since the topic is a very vast one, it was decided to concentrate on the child rearing practices during the early years from birth to five years. Hence the selected families were to have atleast one child aged between 0-5 years.

The total sample selected for the present study was hundred. Fifty families from Peddathanda, Nallaguttapalli thanda and fifty families from Chinnathanda were taken purposively.

The variables like income of the family, education of the mother and age of the child were taken to see the association between these variables and child rearing practices.

In the fifty traditional Sugali families selected for the study, 15 children are in age range of 0-1 year, 17 are 1-3 years and 18 are 3-5 years. Nineteen of these families have annual income ranging from Rs.2000–Rs.4000 (Group I). While 31 of them have annual income less than Rs. 2000 (Group II). Regarding education of the mother, 45 are illiterates and 5 are literates.

Among fifty transitional Sugali sample families, 22 children are in age-group of 0-1 year, 16 are 1-3 years and 12 are 3-5 years. Thirty three of these families have annual income of Rs.2000–Rs.4000 (Group I). While 17 families have annual income less than Rs. 2000 (Group II) Seventeen are illiterate mothers and 33 are literates.

Tools and Techniques of the Study

The investigator selected interview as the technique for securing information from the subjects (mothers). The interview method was opted because it is possible to develop better understanding through the face to face contact and it also has the additional advantages as it provides scope for clearing the doubts or asking for explanation. Sellitz (1964) stated that the interview method is a superior technique of getting information from the interviewed because in an interview there is a possibility of repeating and rephrasing questions to make sure that they are understood. Another advantage of interview is that people are talking which enables them to develop confidence in people and can develop trust in them. Besides, in an interview the investigator also uses observation which is a simple and powerful technique to get the information what is currently happening.

An interview schedule was planned and prepared with care after referring to related research studies. This interview schedule consisted of three parts: 1) General background, 2) Marriage and family, and 3) Child rearing practices.

Under general background, information on family background, house and surroundings, included to describe the sample of the study. Under marriage and family part particulars about the marriage patterns and practices related to pregnancy and child birth were emphasized. Under child rearing practices religious ceremonies performed on child was the first one. It mostly reflected their happiness and acceptance at the arrival of a child. The second one was feeding practices which focussed on breast feeding, weaning practices. The third area was health and hygienic practices which included items like treatment used for diseases, immunizations, and routine cleaning and bathing practices. Disciplinary measures was the fourth unit under this the information related to disciplinary measures used for inculcating desirable traits in children was also gathered. The parental aspirations regarding education was placed as fifth category.

Apart from the information gathered through the interview schedule, the investigator gathered information on the child rearing practices through observation during her visit. The interview in all cases was the mother. The time taken for each interview was about an hour. The interview was conducted in Telugu, since the language is understood both by the investigator and the subjects.

Pilot Study

Pilot study was conducted to see whether the questions really elicited the desired information or not and to make necessary alteration if need be. Moreover it also helped the investigator to find out the time most convenient for the interviewed to carry out the study. The pilot study was conducted on 10 Sugali mothers 5 of whom were from the traditional group and the other 5 were from the transitional group.

Modification of Interview Schedule

During the pilot study, it was found that the investigator could not get all the necessary information with the help of the prepared schedule. The schedule was modified and few more items were added so as to elicit all desired information. With the help of the modified schedule the investigator collected the data.

Time for Collection of Data

During the pilot study it was found that 6 to 9 in the morning and 3 to 6 in the evening were the time most convenient for the mothers to be interviewed. Hence, the investigator decided to contact the mothers during this period for gathering the necessary information. Two months was taken to complete data collection.

Difficulties Faced

During the pilot study when the investigator firs contacted the mothers, some of them were reluctant to respond. The investigator also experienced difficulty in conducting the interview due to inexperience with the tribals. So the investigator decided to approach them through the school teacher of their community. This proved to be highly successful. The teacher cooperated with the investigator and was good enough to explain the purpose of the study and its importance to the target group. From then on, the investigator had no difficulty in getting the cooperation of the Sugali mothers. For the final study the investigator could get the information independently without the teacher.

Statistical Analysis

The statistical difference in child rearing practices of traditional and transitional Sugalis were ascertained through percentages and t-test for proportions. To find out the association between, economic status of the family, education of the mother, age of the child and child rearing practices in traditional and transitional Sugalis, the chi-square test was used.

Limitations

1. It was not possible to make an intensive study of many Sugali thandas geographically situated in various taluks of the district for want of adequate resources and time.

2. The study was confined to 100 Sugali tribe families.

3. Only mothers were interviewed and observed because most of the fathers were not available in the houses at the time of interview.

4. Only mothers with children in the age-group of 0-5 years were included in this study.

Definitions Used

Child rearing: Child rearing as defined by Levin (1957) is a continuous process referring generally to all the interactions between parents and their children.

Traditional Sugalis: Sugalis who maintain their traditional traits with regard to social, economic and cultural and not affected by extraneous influences.

Transitional Sugalis: Sugalis who are in the stage of social transformation as a result of exposure to the changing society.

Literates: Those who are educated upto or above X class.

Illiterates: Those who are not able to read or write.

Classification of families on income basis:

Group I—Families in the annual income range of Rs. 2000 to Rs. 4000

Group II—Families with annual income below Rs. 2000

4
Results and Discussion

The results of the study are presented and discussed in three parts. The first part deals with general information, the second part includes information on marriage and family and the third part examines the child rearing practices among the Sugalis.

General Information

Details of the Sample Families

Table 4.1 shows that out of the fifty families of the traditional Sugalis 92 percent are nuclear and only 8 percent are joint. In the fifty families of transitional Sugalis, 94 percent are nuclear and only 6 percent are joint. A few nuclear families have dependents like widowed mother-in-low.

From the above findings it is found that a majority of the families among the Sugalis of both traditional and transitional are nuclear in nature. In this Sugali community usually the newly married couples move away soon after marriage from their parental family units. Nag (1954) Pandu Ranga Swamy, K. (1983) also reported similar findings among Lambadis of Andhra Pradesh respectively.

Table 4.1 also shows the six of the families of the traditional and transitional Sugalis. It is evident from the table that among the traditional Sugalis, 76 percent of the families consist of 4-6 members each, 24 percent of the families have 7-9 members each.

Among the Sugalis in transition, 54 percent of the families include 1-3 members each, 32 percent of the families have 4-6 members each and only 14 percent of the families consist of 7-9 members each.

Among the traditional Sugalis, 80 percent are primarily cultivators and collectors and sellers of firewood and the remaining 20 percent are mainly agricultural labourers. During agricultural seasons, these agricultural labourers often migrate for short periods of time to other places where there is a lot of farming activity. As a secondary occupation, almost all the traditional Sugalis engage in collecting forest produce like seasonal fruits, soap-nuts, broomsticks and honey. The items collected are sold or bartered in the weekly shandy. Some of them have taken to cattle-rearing as a secondary occupation. Some Sugali women take up embroidery work to earn wages.

Among the families of the Sugalis in transition, 66 percent are primarily dependent on different jobs such as primary school teachers, watchman, attenders and clerks and secondarily on agriculture. The remaining 34 percent are primarily agriculturists and secondarily agricultural labourers.

Thus a vast majority of the traditional Sugalis are mainly agriculturists but bulk of the Sugalis in transition are primarily dependent on non-agricultural activities.

Table 4.1 shows the distribution of the Sugalis by income. Even though, the traditional Sugalis and those in transition are working hard, their income level is still below the poverty line. In the traditional Sugalis 38 percent of the families have an annual income between Rs. 2000/- to 4000/- (Group I) and 62 percent of the families are having an annual income of below Rs. 2000/- (Group II). In the transitional Sugalis 66 percent of the families have an annual income between Rs. 2000/- to 4000/- (Group I) and 34 percent of the families have an annual income of below Rs. 2000/- (Group II).

The above findings indicate that the annual income of a majority of the traditional Sugalis is below Rs. 2000/- but the annual income of a majority of the transitional Sugalis is more than Rs. 2000/-

Table 4.1 further shows the percentage distribution of the Sugali families by their education. With reference to education of the parents, 64 percent of the fathers and 90 percent of the mothers are illiterates and only 36 percent of the fathers and 10 percent of the mothers are literates among the traditional Sugalis. On the contrary among the Sugalis in transition, 32 percent of the fathers and 34 percent of the mothers are illiterates. While 68 percent of the fathers and 66 percent of the mothers are literates.

It is observed that many of the parents in traditional Sugali group are illiterates. Hence there is a need to organise adult education programmes for men and women in a more intensive manner.

Table 4.1 : Details about Family Background of the Sample Families

Particulars of the Family	Traditional Sugalis		Transitional Sugalis	
	No.	%	No.	%
Type				
Nuclear	46	92	47	94
Joint	4	8	3	6
Number of Members				
1–3	---	---	27	54
4–6	38	76	16	32
7–9	12	24	7	14
Annual Income				
Rs. 2000/- to 4000/- (Group I)	19	38	33	66
Below Rs. 2000/- (Group II)	31	62	17	34
Education of the Parents				
Illiterates				
Fathers	32	64	16	32
Mothers	45	90	17	34
Literates				
Fathers	18	36	34	68
Mothers	5	10	33	66

House and Surroundings

It is found that 82 percent of the traditional Sugalis stay in single room circular huts with conical roofing. The remaining 18 percent live in tiled-roof houses each with two or three rooms. Almost 25 percent of the families have cattle sheds attached to their houses. Most of their houses provide little privacy for the inmates. Cleanliness, lighting and maintenance of all houses are poor.

In transitional Sugali group, 12 percent of them live in single room circular huts with conical roofing, 26 percent live in tiled-roof houses each consisting of two or three rooms and the remaining 62 percent live in houses with reinforced concrete roofs which have been donated to them by the Social Welfare Department of the Government of Andhra Pradesh. Only 8 percent of the houses with tiled roofs have cattle sheds attached to them. A majority of the houses owned by the Sugalis in transition have more than one room and provide privacy to some extent for the inmates. Moreover the housing conditions regarding cleanliness, lighting and maintenance are satisfactory.

Water Facilities

The Peddathanda and Nallaguttapalli thanda area inhabited by the traditional Sugalis have two bore wells each. All the inhabitants collect water from the nearby borewell whenever necessary. On the other hand, the Chinnathanda inhabited by the Sugalis in transition has one bore well and one open well. Neither the traditional Sugalis nor the transitional Sugalis face water problem in their respective settlements.

Sanitation

The traditional type of Sugali thandas are lacking proper drainage facilities around the houses. Each house lets out its waste water into a soakage pit. When the pit gets full the water overflows and spreads allover the place making the thandas dirty. Cattle are kept in cattle sheds attached to the houses, these also are not cleaned frequently. Apart from this, children use the open places near their houses for toilet purposes and it is not disposed off properly. All these make the sanitation in the traditional Sugali thandas very poor.

In the traditional Sugali thanda, the drainage facilities such as covered soakage pits are provided by the Government. Very few of them have cattle sheds attached to their houses. Even though some of the children use the open places around the houses for toilet purposes, it is cleaned immediately. As a result the sanitation is satisfactory when compared to traditional Sugali thandas.

Household Possessions

The families of the traditional Sugalis use mostly earthern were and to some extent metalware as cooking utensils. Many families have adequate number of earthern posts meant for domestic purposes. They use mate, old clothes or bed sheets as bedding materials. Infants under two months are put in a bamboo cradle into which several old clothes are spread. After two months of age, children are put in usual hanging cradles made of old clothes or gunny bags. As majority of the parents are illiterates, they have no necessity of keeping writing materials like table, chair, paper, pen/pencils with them. Almost every family owns a radio. None of them gets news papers or magazines to read. All of them use traditional type of dress, costumes, accessories and cosmetics. Gold ornaments like ear rings and nose rings are worn by some of the women. More than 60 percent of the women posses silver ornaments. No commercial toys are made available to the children. Empty tins, small size cooking vessels, spoons, lids etc., are used as toys for the pre-school children.

Like the traditional Sugalis, a few Sugalis in transition also use earthern pots. However a great majority of the transitional Sugali families own more cooking vessels made of metal. Some of these families also posses cots, mattresses, pillows apart from the traditional mats and bed sheets. For children, mothers make hanging cradles with bedsheets or old sarees/dhotis and hang it from the roof as seen in other communities. A majority of the transitional Sugalis are literates and give importance to writing and reading materials and utilize furniture like table, chair, for the purpose. During leisure periods they spend their leisure time by reading magazines or newspapers and listening to radio programmes. It is observed that the transitional group of Sugalis do not use traditional type of dresses, costumes, accessories and cosmetics. Besides indigenous types, very few families possess commercial toys such as plastic balls, rubber dolls, wooden toys etc., for their children to play. A few of them own cycles and watches.

The above findings indicate that the life style of the Sugalis in transition is similar to the Hindus in their neighbourhood.

Marriage and Family

Marriage particulars

The data presented in Table 4.2 shows that 36 percent of

traditional Sugali women got married before reaching 16 years of age but after attaining menarche. The remaining (64%) were found to marry at the age of 16-18 years. None of the traditional Sugali men were noticed to marry before reaching 16 years of age. Thirty eight percent of the men got married between the age of 16-18 years and the rest (62%) between the age of 18-20 years.

Table 4.2 : Distribution of Sugali Women and Men by Age at Marriage

Age at Marriage	Traditional Group				Transitional Group			
	Women		Men		Women		Men	
	No.	%	No.	%	No.	%	No.	%
Below 16 years	18	36	--	--	9	18	--	--
16–18 years	32	64	19	38	24	48	7	14
18–20 years	--	--	30	60	11	22	29	58
20–22 years	--	--	1	2	6	12	14	28
Total	50	100	50	100	50	100	50	100

Among the transitional Sugalis, 18 percent of the women got married before 16 years but after menarche, 48 percent between 16-18 years, 22 percent between 18-20 years and the rest (12%) between 20-22 years. Regarding Sugali men in the transitional group, none of them were found to marry before reaching 16 years. Fourteen percent of the men got married between 16-18 years, 58 percent between 18-20 years and 28 percent between 20-22 years.

From the above findings, it is evident that generally Sugali girls are not married before puberty. Earlier studies on tribals by different research workers shown similar finding. Vyas's, N.N. (1970) study on Bhils, Basu's, M.P. (1970) study on Banjaras, Naik's, S. and Sharma's, A.K. (1985) study on Bhuiyans.

Rao, M. (1985) reports that age at marriage is always negatively correlated with number of children. The younger the woman at marriage, the more will be the conceptions. Hence physiological and nutritional stress may be more among these women. A majority of the traditional Sugali women are observed to have early marriages than transitional Sugali women. The age at marriage of Sugali men is also increased from traditional to transitional group. This rising trend with regard to age at the time of marriage from traditional to transitional Sugalis may be due to increase in education levels.

Seventy six percent of the traditional and 62 percent of the transitional Sugalis had arranged marriages. Twenty four percent of the traditional and 38 percent of the transitional Sugalis had love marriages. In arranged marriages, parents or elders select the marriage partner for their children and settle the terms and conditions for marriage following the formalities, customs and practices prevalent in the community. This might be done with or without consulting the bride or bridegroom. In love marriages, the young boy and girl fall in love with each other and decide to marry. They might or might not inform their parents about their decision before performing the marriage.

It is of interest to note that almost all the marriages (92%) in traditional group are found to be consanguineous type. Whereas in transitional group 78 percent are observed to be consanguineous marriages. A decreasing trend in the proportion of consanguineous marriages have been observed from traditional to transitional Sugalis and this may be due to cross-cultural contacts and other influences of urbanisation.

Out of the consanguineous marriages observed in both the groups majority (86%) of the marriages are materilateral cross-cousin marriages (Fa Si So- Mo Br Da) and rest of them are uncle-niece marriages.

Pandu Ranga Swamy's, K. (1983) study on Sugalis of Kurnool district, Andhra Pradesh, reported that matrilateral cross-cousin marriages are mostly seen in that group. Even in the present study also it is true.

On the whole the consanguinity rate is high for the tribals in Andhra Pradesh. From the literature it is noticed that many tribal communities like Koya, Gond Naga, Yerukula, Sugali, Chenchu, Irular, Nakkala, Totos practice consanguineous marriages and almost all the tribals have custom of matrilateral cross-cousin marriages except in Chenchu tribe, who have practice of uncle-niece marriages.

A majority of the Sugalis (62%) in traditional group had selected their spouses from within their thanda or from nearby thandas situated at a distance of about 1 to 2 kilometers away. The reason may be that they want to marry the persons who are known personally. On the other hand, 68 percent of the transitional Sugalis had selected their spouses from outside their thanda from places about five or six kilometers away.

Particulars About Pregnancy

Among the traditional group, a majority (92%) of the women have had less than a year of gap between marriage and birth of first child. In the transitional group, it observed in nearly half of the proportion of women. Rest of them, 38 percent and 12 percent had 1-2 years and 2-4 years gap respectively.

From the above findings it is noticed that from traditional to transitional Sugali women, the gap between marriage and birth of the first child is raised. In both the groups the women have not used any family planning methods to maintain gap purposively. It also shows that the fertility rate is high among traditional women compared to transitional women.

It is found that most of the women in traditional group (72%) were not fully aware of the pregnancy symptoms. If the women miss the menstrual cycle for two or three consecutive months and have some other minor signs like vomiting, desire for special foods appear then they disclose to mother-in-laws or elderly women and get conform themselves. Eighty percent of the transitional women were observed to be aware of the pregnancy symptoms fully and they revealed this event to their husbands first. This difference with regard to lack of awareness of pregnancy symptoms may be due to high occurrence of early marriages in traditional group.

Sixty four percent of the traditional and 76 percent of the transitional women had given birth to their first child at the natal home. Rest of the women in both the groups had given birth to their first child at their homes itself. It is also noticed that there is no binding for the next consecutive delivery and it is a matter of one's convenience.

Pregnancy Taboos

It is significant to note that among tribals every aspect of life from birth to death were marked by specific customs, beliefs and notions which are practiced in their day-to-day life. (Jaiswal, 1977). Among the Sugalis, certain pregnancy taboos relating to food, movement, sexual practices are observed.

Ninety six percent of the traditional and 98 percent of the transitional women are restricted against eating papaya during pregnancy. The reason is that it is believed to cause abortions. The practice is also found in other communities of South India (Rajyalakshmi, 1969). Black fruits like berries, neredu fruits (Myrtus Cyminum Rox) grapes, nuts etc. are avoided by 46 percent of traditional and 38 percent of transitional women. The reason expressed by them for the taboo are that 'Nalla Chevva' (Nalla=Black; Chevva=Disease) will occur and child will be born black in colour if mother eat black coloured fruits during pregnancy. Eggs were tabooed by 30 percent of traditional and 28 percent of transitional women, as eggs are believed to cause flatulence and heat. Roots and tubers specially potato is not eaten by pregnant women of traditional (28%) and transitional (22%) groups. The reason behind it is that potato is believed to result in flatus particularly in children and nursing mothers. The similar belief is prevalent with regard to pumpkin and so 10 percent of traditional and 6 percent of transitional women avoided them. Some of the other foods like jaggery, groundnuts, bengalgram dhal are also restricted because they are believed to heat up the body systems and produce flatus in children.

The causes for avoiding majority of the foods are observed to be wrong concepts and beliefs among the tribal mothers (Vimala and Ratnaprabha, unpublished). From the nutritional point of view avoidance of foods during pregnancy can cause more damage to the nutritional status of mother which may inturn affect the child's health.

Visiting burial ground is avoided by 94 percent of the traditional and 84 percent of the transitional pregnant women. Visiting temple uphills is restricted by 72 percent of the traditional and 66 percent of the transitional Sugali women. Doing strenuous work is tabooed by 28 percent of the traditional and 24 percent of the transitional women. Travelling after dusk is restricted for traditional (16%) and transitional (14%) women. Long walk also is one of the taboo which is practiced by 16 percent of the traditional and 12 percent of the transitional women. Seeing a dead body is also a taboo by 64 percent of the traditional and 60 percent of the transitional Sugali women.

If the above said movement taboos during pregnancy are not followed properly, they believe that will be complicated delivery and that they will have harmful effects on babies. Visiting burial ground and seeing a dead body are particularly tabooed as it is believed that some evil spirits which hover these places will do harm to the mother as well as to the baby in the womb.

The purpose of these movement taboos are not to strain the women and to keep women emotionally well during pregnancy. Traditional Sugalis (40%) and transitional sugalis (32%) have sexual taboo during pregnancy. This taboo on intercourse should last for five months after the birth of the baby. The reason given for the custom is that intercourse will make the mother's milk bad and cause the baby to become unhealthy. By observing the six of the families in traditional Sugalis, this taboo seem to be not practiced properly.

Apart from the above mentioned taboos, some other taboos are also observed by the Sugalis include the following:

1. The pregnant women should not allow a sparrow to fly over her. If it happens, it is believed that after birth the baby will be very weak until some magician drives off.

2. The pregnant women should stay indoors during eclipses, otherwise there will be some physical malformations of the baby when it is born.

3. The dog should not cross a pregnant women, as it will affect her child's limbs which can be cured only by a magician. It is noticed that all the taboos are applicable to all the pregnancies of Sugali women.

Special Foods During Pregnancy

One of the most interesting phenomena during pregnancy is 'cravings'- the irresistible longing of an expectant mother for a particular item of food. Among the traditional Sugalis, 84 percent of the women had cravings for special foods during first pregnancy. The foods mentioned were specific fruits (62%), specific berries (52%) specific non-vegetarian foods (50%) and specific sweets (34%).

Among the transitional Sugalis, 96 percent of the women had cravings for the following special foods during first pregnancy were specific fruits (80%), specific berries (62%), specific non-vegetarian foods (84%) and specific sweets (56%).

It is observed from the data that a greater proportion of women in the transitional group expressed cravings for special items during pregnancy. It is interesting to note that the specific fruits and berries which are desired by traditional and transitional Sugali women are easily available in forests and hills. Most of the non-vegetarian foods (goat, chicken, meat) are also available from hunting. Specific sweet desired is mainly payasam prepared with rice flour and jaggery. Besides these the transitional women are found to prefer pokodas, laddus etc.

Among the traditional group, 62 percent of the women received special foods during first pregnancy only. In the transitional group, 74 percent of the women received special foods during first as well as in subsequent pregnancies. The husband or mother-in-law were reported to supply the same. Swaroop, R. (1963) reported that the cravings are regarded as sacred wishes among certain primitive tribes.

Ceremonies Performed During Pregnancy

In traditional group, it is observed that two ceremonies are performed when women conceive for the first time. The process of performing the ceremonies are as follows: At sixth or seventh months, girl's father, mother along with some elderly relatives come to the house on an auspicious day. They bring sweets, fruits, flowers, new saree to the daughter and perform the puja to Munidevara. Then a feast is arranged. Rice, mutton curry, payasam are special items for the feast. In the thanda, one member from each family will be invited to the feast. In the evening they drink and dance. Another ceremony takes place during the ninth month of pregnancy. On that day they prepare rice and rasam with crabs as it is a favourite dish for them. They invite all the relatives and elders in the thanda. The pregnant lady also eats with them then they end up the ceremony with drink and dance.

In transitional group, the above mentioned ceremonies are not customarily practiced; to minimise the expenditure. Moreover the customs and practices which are prevalent in traditional group are slowly disappearing in transitional group due to urbanization and contact with non-tribal communities.

Particulars About Confinement

Among the traditional Sugalis, 94 percent of the women have had home deliveries and a very few (6%) had been taken to Maternity hospital when they experienced difficulties in child birth. Almost all the deliveries were attended by elderly women in the thanda. A few families (12%) called a local dai (village mid wife) when the women had unbearable pains and the labour was prolonged.

Among the transitional Sugalis, 66 percent of the women have had home deliveries, 26 percent in Maternity hospital and 8 percent in private hospitals. A majority of the deliveries (84%) were reported normal. Only 6 percent and 10 percent of the deliveries are seen as forceps and caesarian respectively. Though more than half of the transitional women had home deliveries, a local dai was present in many cases (46%) besides an elderly women.

According to India population Project-II (1981) it is noted that a vast majority of deliveries in Andhra Pradesh took place at home. The findings is found to be true in the case of the traditional Sugalis.

From the foregoing details it is evident that the transitional Sugalis are getting awareness towards utilization of medical services available, because they live nearer to urban centres. Such a facility may not be available for the traditional group. Moreover they are mostly illiterates and traditional in their thinking. They may therefore resort to home deliveries.

Regarding birth spacing, 98 percent of the traditional women were found to have 1-2 years gap between children while the rest had a gap of 2-4 years, whereas in transitional group, 62 percent of the women found to have 1-2 years gap between children while the rest (38%) had a gap of 2-4 years.

From the above data, it is evident that there is less spacing between conceptions in the traditional when compared to transitional group. Due to increase in education and awareness towards medical services the Sugali women under transition are maintaining birth spacing to improve the health of the mother and child.

In traditional group, 10 percent of the women expressed health complaints during first pregnancy. At the time of third and fourth pregnancies, 22 percent of them were reported to be unhealthy. This may be due to less gap between conceptions. Birth spacing have a revolutionary impact on both maternal and child health. Hence there is a need to educate women to maintain proper health by adopting family planning.

In transitional group, majority of the women (92%) expressed that there are no health complaints during pregnancies. Only 8 percent reported about anemia, toxemia etc. in third and fourth pregnancies.

Particulars About Abortions

Abortions are two types: 1. Spontaneous which can be due to natural causes, and 2. Induced, voluntarily. Among the traditional and transitional Sugalis 22 percent of the women had 1-2 abortions. Fourteen percent of traditional and 6 percent of transitional Sugali women had spontaneous abortions during second and third months of pregnancy. The rest of the women in the traditional (8%) and transitional (16%) group had induced abortion in the third or fourth months of pregnancy.

From the above findings it is noticed that higher number of spontaneous abortions occurred in traditional women than transitional women. The causes for this may be heavy work, lack of special care during pregnancy, inadequate nutrition, frequent of deliveries.

In relation to induced abortions, the number is increased more among the transitional Sugali women as compared to the traditional group. In the traditional group, 62 percent of the women have not undergone terminal methods of family planning due to fear about sterilization operation. As a result, they go for induced abortions to stop the unwanted child births. On the other hand, in the transitional group, the women have gone for induced abortions mainly to maintain spacing between pregnancies (2–4 years).

M.T.P. Act was introduced to legitimatise abortion and make sure that no unwanted children are added to families. According to Part (1980) in India, the incidence of abortion is about 6 million, out of which 4 million are induced and 2 million spontaneous.

In traditional Sugali group, the method proposed to get induced abortion is through herbal medicines i.e., a mixture of extracts from 'jajikaya', 'jamakaya', 'marrikaya', 'vamu' and 'kasthuri' tablets called locally 'Kasayamu'. Whereas in transitional group the method used to get induced abortion is through Government or private hospitals.

Number of Children for-Ideal Family

It is observed that none of the traditional Sugali women considered a family of only one or two children to be ideal. Twenty six percent of them reported that having three children is ideal. More than half of the respondents (56%) expressed that a family consisting four children as ideal. Rest of them (18%) considered five children as the ideal numbers.

In the transitional Sugali group, 14 percent of the women expressed ideal family size as consisting of one child. Fifty eight percent reported that having two children as ideal, 18 percent of them mentioned three children as ideal and remaining (10%) considered four children as ideal.

It is clearly understood that in traditional group, a significantly higher proportion of women (56%) considered to have four or more children as ideal family. In transitional group, 58 percent of the women expressed that having two children as ideal family. Thus it is noticed that larger family size is reported as ideal by traditional Sugali women. Freedman and Whelpton (1950) stated that "the person who adhere to traditional ideas in general will also adhere to traditional ideas about fertility planning and family size." The traditional Sugali women reported to get three types of utility from large number of children.

(1) a source of supplement in the family income;

(2) as a potential source of security either in old age or as and when necessity arises;

(3) as a source of personal pleasure.

The foregoing details shows that a majority of the women in traditional group desire to have large six (4 or 5 children) families. Fear of losing children is a main cause for their desire to have more children (Dave, C. et al 1981). Greater proportion of women in transitional Sugali group are desirous of having small size (2 or 3 children) families. As majority of transitional Sugalis are literates, education has an impact on family size. Moreover, the propaganda for smaller families which has been much publicized through the numerous 'family planning' programmes seem to have made a impact on the parents of this group.

Number of Children Presented

Table 4.3 reveals that among the traditional group, 12 percent of the families have 1–2 children 82 percent of them have 3–4 children and 6 percent have more than 4 children.

Among the transitional group, 16 percent of the families are found to have 1-2 children, 60 percent of them have 3-4 children and very few (4%) have more than 4 children.

Table 4.3 : Number of Children Presented

Number of Children	Traditional Group		Transitional Group	
	No.	%	No.	%
1–2	6	12	18	36
3–4	41	82	30	60
More than 4	3	6	2	4
Total	*50*	*100*	*50*	*100*

The above findings reveal that the majority of traditional Sugali families consist of three or four children compared to transitional Sugali families. Due to early marriages in traditional group, there is a possibility to have more number of conceptions and they are under the belief that the child birth is the grace and gift of God; it is the destiny to have the large number of children. This trend is also seen in Yanadi tribe of Andhra Pradesh (Gurumurthy, G. (1984).

As a majority of the traditional Sugalis are illiterates, they have shown preference for more number of children when compared to transitional Sugalis. The study by Dave, C. and Sadashivaiah, K. (1981) also revealed that when both couples are educated they prefer small family. Education is the most important factor in improving the quality of family life.

Sex Preference

The most predominant theme in the Indian Epics and literature is the birth of a son. Many emphasize that the begetting of a son is one of man's highest duties and the only way through which he can discharge the debt he owes to his ancestors. This preference for a son is as old as Indian society itself.

In the present investigation, it is noticed that a large majority of respondents (94%) in traditional group indicated a preference for a son as eldest child. Only a few (4%) of them reported desire to have a girl as first child. The rest (2%) reported to have a child of either sex (Table 4.4).

Table 4.4 : Sex Preference of the First Child

Particulars	Traditional Group		Transitional Group	
	No.	%	No.	%
Preferred Sex of the First Child :				
Boy	47	94	33	66
Girl	2	4	12	24
Any one	1	2	5	10
Total	50	100	50	100

In transitional group, 66 percent of the women were observed to show preference for a son as first child. Twenty four percent for a girl as first child and 10% for either male or female child.

As Mac Donell (1976) stated the traditional preference for sons is still very much intact in India. It is found that preference for a son as first child is more among traditional Sugalis than transitional Sugalis. On the whole greater preference for a son is seen in both the groups. The reasons for preference for sons expressed by them are as follows: 1) they are responsible for the perpetuation of the family name; 2) sons take the responsibility of looking after parents in old age; 3) parents feel that sons are great asset to help in their work; 4) son can perform all religious rites. The similar reasons for preference of sons are expressed on Lahiri's, S. (1974) study.

In an attitude survey carried out in Bombay in 1970's by the International Institute for population studies (IIPS), it was found that some respondents describing three children initially and clarified later, that they were willing to extend their family size even to nine in order to ensure a male child. This situation is found to be true mostly in traditional Sugali families.

Sinha's, U.P. (1984) study concluded that in the tribal society female children are relatively well cared for and thus the female child experience greater longevity than males. In the present study, even though very few of them preferred girl as the first child, it is increased from traditional to transitional group. They stated that girls are preferred because they could give help to mothers in domestic work. Some of them considered the girl as Lakshmidevi (a Goddess of wealth) and considered that it would be prosperous for them if the eldest one is a girl. Few of them expressed that female children will bring bride price for their parents at the time of marriage.

Subjects were asked to indicate the sex preference for subsequent children. Table 5.5 shows that a majority of the respondents (44%) in traditional group preferred a girl as subsequent child provided the first was a son. Other 52 percent of the women preferred a child of either sex. Very few of them (4%) indicated preference for boy as a subsequent child.

Table 4.5 : Sex Preference of the Subsequent Children

Particulars	Traditional Group		Transitional Group	
	No.	%	No.	%
Preferred Sex of the Subsequent Children:				
Boy	2	4	1	2
Girl	23	44	20	40
Any one	26	52	29	58
Total	*50*	*100*	*50*	*100*

In transitional group, 40 percent of the women preferred girl as subsequent child. Either boy or girl is preferred by 58 percent of the women. Very few (2%) preferred boy as a subsequent child.

A majority of the women in both the groups are found to prefer girls as subsequent children if the first borns are boys. Nearly more than half of them in both the groups did not indicate a special preference for subsequent children.

Method Used to Limit Family Size

With respect to the awareness of family planning method it is clear that in the traditional group, a considerable number (70%) shows awareness towards vasectomy and tubectomy. Knowledge about local methods of family planning like use of herbal medicines are indicated by 22 percent of the women.

In the transitional group, 62 percent of the women were aware of induced abortions as a birth control measures and 88 percent of them also known about terminal methods of family planning. Fourty-six percent of them knew also about a abstinence, withdrawal, condoms, oral contraceptives, intrauterine devices such as loops etc.

Among the traditional Sugalis, 62 percent of the men and women had not yet undergone sterilization operations to stop the child births. Only 38 percent of them are proposed to adopt terminal methods of family planning. It is also interesting to note that out of 38 percent of the respondents who had undergone sterilization, 34 percent were women and only 4 percent were men.

Among the transitional Sugalis, 36 percent of the people had not used any family planning method. The other 64 percent of the Sugalis used contraceptive measures. Out of 64 percent of the respondents, 30 percent of the women proposed to undergo tubectomy operations, 16 percent of the women are found to use temporary methods of IUD, oral contraceptives etc. and 18 percent of the men proposed to undergo vasectomy operation.

From the above findings it is observed that a majority of traditional Sugalis have not yet accepted and undergone birth control measures. Basu, M.P. (1967) also found the same trend among Banjaras of Andhra Pradesh.

It is evident that a majority of the women in both the traditional and transitional Sugali groups had undergone tubectomy operation. Though transitional Sugali women were aware of pills, loops, condoms, most of them were not using them.

A majority of the men and women in traditional Sugali group are afraid about sterilization, they also considered it as a sin to undergo sterilization and they desire to have more children particularly male children. In transitional Sugali group these fears are reduced and they showed a preference for sterilization. The percentage of people who use contraceptive devices are increased from traditional transitional group may be due to their educational status, mass-media influence and urbanization.

Thirty percent of the traditional Sugalis are motivated by village health worker to adopt family planning methods. Twenty two percent of them by elders in thandas, 4 percent of them by doctors, and 6 percent of them got motivated towards it through advertisements in radio.

In transitional group, 52 percent of them are motivated to adopt family planning methods by village health workers. Thirty two percent by elders, 28 percent by doctors, 14 percent by radio programmes and 10 percent by reading the magazines.

Government has been provided monitory incentives i.e., Rs.120 per person who adopt sterilization.

Among the traditional Sugalis, 86 percent of the families have radio or transistor but they are not able to use it properly due to lack of time. It is found that 86 percent of them reported to listen to music, 28 percent to listen to Farmer's forum and only one family (2%) to listen to news and educational programmes on different topics.

Among the transitional Sugalis, 88 percent of the families owned radio or transistor. Almost all of them are found to listen to film songs. Fourty percent to Farmer's forum, 30 percent to news, 26 percent to nutrition and health programmes and 16 percent to women and child welfare programmes.

Thus it is clear that in traditional Sugali group, as most of the people are illiterates, they find it difficult to follow the educational programmes, Masani (1976) also made a similar observations. Education helps to determine a mother's exposure to new information and makes both more willing and able to take advantage of new thinking and innovations. Thus it is clear that in transitional group, since most of them are literates, they have given importance to educational programmes and they are able to derive benefits from the farmer's programmes.

Though radio holds a high potential as a mass-medium of education, the messages broadcasted are not reaching the target group especially traditional tribals due to lack of interest, motivation, and ability to understanding the programme.

Another important mass-media available is newspapers and magazines. But only two families (4%) in traditional and 8 families (16%) in transitional group are found to buy the newspapers and magazines. In traditional group, all of them are reading film news and stories. In transitional group, 10 percent of them are reading information about nutrition and health, 10 percent about women and child welfare, 2 percent about news and 16 percent about film news and stories.

From the above data it is observed that as majority of the traditional Sugalis who are mostly illiterates are not reading the newspaper and magazines when compared to transitional Sugalis.

Child Rearing Practices

This part presents the findings of the child raring practices, specifically the areas like religious ceremonies performed on children, feeding practices, health and hygienic practices, disciplinary measures and parental educational aspirations for the children in traditional Sugalis and the Sugalis in transition. In this context t-test is used to know the significant differences between the child-rearing practices of the two categories of Sugalis. Chi-square test is used to know the association between the variables like income level, education of the mother, age of the child and child rearing practices of the groups of Sugalis under study.

Religious Ceremonies Performed on Children

The concern of the Indian people for the upbringing of children dates back over many centuries. Grihya Sutras, the ancient Hindu sacred texts, contain 'Samskaras' as concepts in child rearing practices. These religious ceremonies deal with many stages in an infant's life emerging from conception to the age of six. Sound mental health is believed to be dependent on the way a child has been reared in his childhood.

The traditional and transitional Sugalis perform the following religious ceremonies after the birth of a child.

Purificatory Ceremony

Purificatory ceremony is performed on the fourth day after child-birth. Almost two thirds (62%) of the traditional and less than half (42%) of the transitional Sugali families performed this ceremony. This shows a significant difference ($p < 0.05$).

After giving birth to a child, a Sugali mother is considered impure for three days. She remains in a hut specially set apart for her. On the fourth day, she and her child are given a ceremonial bath after anointing their body with gingelly oil mixed with turmeric. After the bath, the mother along with her child reaches a pit dug in front of the house, puts ten paise coins in that pit and worships tribal Goddesses at the pit with turmeric, vemilion flowers and three kinds of grains. Then the mother waters the trees located nearby and washes the feet of the children. Then she offers food to ancestors. Sweets made with rice flour and jaggery are distributed amongst the children. Thereafter the mother returns home. The guests are entertained to a feast in which rice, wheat cakes, mutton and payasam made with rice flour and jaggery are served.

The purpose of purificatory ceremony is to provide cleanliness and resistance power against infectious diseases.

Bahadur, K.P. (1977) reported that among the Banjaras also the process is similar but the ceremony is performed on the fifth day after delivery.

Ceremony if Male Child is Born

Among the Sugalis sons are preferred to daughters. Dramatic demonstration of this preference for sons is "highlighted by the performance of an elaborate birth ceremony at the time of birth of a son. On an auspicious day after the birth of a son, a feast is arranged in which strong drinks are served and then the guests are entertained by a dance. Both the groups of Sugalis shows equal interest in performing this ceremony. In fact 68 percent of the traditional Sugali families and 62 percent of the transitional Sugali families performed this ceremony. Among the Amat Gonds tribe also this ceremony was performed with great enthusiasm (Dube, L. 1949).

Cradling Ceremony

Cradling ceremony is performed on the purificatory day. The baby is placed in a cradle which is made from a basket with old clothes spread on its floor. The baby talcum powder, eye cream, soap etc. are kept below the old clothes put into a cradle. This ceremony was performed by 38 percent and 46 percent of the traditional and transitional Sugali families respectively. This shows no significant difference statistically between the two groups.

Name-giving Ceremony

Name-giving ceremony is performed either on the 12th day after delivery or on an auspicious day after one month of the delivery. Until the performance of this ceremony the mother and the baby are given bath twice a day, in the morning and evening. On the name-giving day all the members of the household take bath and the house is cleaned. The mother smears the scalp of the child with a mixture of singly oil and turmeric powder, gives him bath with warm water and enrobes the child with the new clothes brought by the child's maternal uncle. Then the parents name the child as per the direction of the priest. This practice is also seen in the Ollar tribe of Orissa (Jha, M. 1963). If the parents have already taken a vow to name the child after some deity the child is named only after that deity. Most of the traditional Sugalis select some of their ancestor's names or that of the local deities. Mundri's, L.S. (1956) study also revealed the same finding in Munda tribe, Bihar. Aphale, C. (1976) found that in Poona the names of gods were favoured more by the illiterate or slightly educated families which belonged to intermediate and scheduled castes. On the other hand most of the Sugalis in transition give modern names to their children. Twenty six percent of the traditional and 22 percent of the transitional Sugali families performed name giving ceremony. This also shows that the two groups do not differ significantly in this aspect.

These cradling and name giving ceremonies are performed on child to accept him as a member of the family.

Tonsure Ceremony

The traditional Sugalis offer their children's hair either to their household deities (ilevelpu devudu) namely Ankalamma, Hingalamma, and Maramma or to the Hindu Gods like Venkateswara etc. When their children reach one year or two years of age, they offer their children's hair to the respective deities after sacrificing a sheep or a goat to those deities. On that day they invite their relatives to a feast.

A majority of the transitional Sugalis offer their child's hair to Lord Venkateswara whom they call Balaji rather than to their traditional deities. It may be either because of the less religiosity and faith in tribal Goddesses or because of the greater influence of Hinduism (Srinivas, 1962).

The significance for tonsure ceremony is to get good hair and health after removing the birth-hair. Sixty six percent of the traditional and 68 percent of the transitional Sugali families performed the tonsure ceremony.

The foregoing details reveal that unlike the Sugalis in transition majority of the traditional Sugalis are found to perform purificatory ceremony. However both the groups of Sugalis celebrate special ceremonies to mark the birth of a son.

Table 4.6 : Performance of Religious Ceremonies for Children by Sugalis

Name of the Ceremony	Sugali Groups		t-Value
	Traditional	Transitional	
Purificatory Ceremony	62 (31)	42 (21)	2.06*
Ceremony associated with birth of a male child	68 (34)	62 (31)	0.64
Cradling ceremony	38 (19)	46 (23)	0.82
Name Giving Ceremony	26 (13)	22 (11)	0.48
Tonsure Ceremony	66 (33)	68 (34)	0.21

* Indicates significant difference at 0.05 level of significance
t Table value 2.58 at 0.01 level of significance
t table value 1.96 at 0.05 level of significance
Figures in parentheses denotes number

Table 4.7 clearly shows the association between the income and education of the mother and performance of ceremonies on children. The traditional Sugali families with higher income (Group-I) perform more ceremonies than the traditional Sugali families with lower income (Group II). This shows that there is significant association between income and performance of ceremonies (p<0.01). Unlike the literate mothers, majority of the illiterate mothers in the traditional group are found to perform the ceremonies.

Among the transitional Sugalis no significant association is found between income of families and the performance of ceremonies on children. However, a significant relationship (p<0.01) is noticed between education of the mother and the ceremonies performed for children.

Feeding Practices

Feeding practices are so intertwined with the culture and value

Table 4.7 : Distribution of the Traditional and Transitional Sugali Mothers According to Income of the Family, Education of the Mother and Ceremonies Performed on Children

Income and education levels of the Sugalis	Purificatory ceremony		Special ceremony for male child		Cradling ceremony		Name ceremony		Tonsure ceremony		X²-Value
	No.	%	No.	%	No.	%	No.	%	No.	%	
1. Traditional											
Group I	16	84.2	17	89.4	12	63.1	10	52.6	13	68.4	26.34**
Group II	15	48.3	17	54.8	7	22.5	3	9.67	20	64.5	
Illiterate Mothers	29	64.4	33	73.3	18	40.0	11	24.4	32	71.1	
Literate Mothers	2	40.0	1	20.0	1	20.0	2	40.0	1	20.0	
2. Transitional											
Group I	12	36.3	24	72.7	18	54.5	9	27.2	23	69.6	9.73
Group II	9	52.9	7	41.1	5	29.4	2	11.7	11	64.7	
Illiterate Mothers	15	88.2	11	64.7	16	94.1	8	47.0	12	70.5	48.39**
Literate Mothers	6	18.1	20	60.6	7	21.2	3	9.0	22	66.7	

** Indicates significant association at 0.01 level of significance.

system, that changes in one area are bound to influenced or occasioned by changes in the other.

Initiation of Breast Feeding

By initiating breast feeding early the practice of giving prelacteal feeds, which is deleterious to the infant can be avoided. Also the infant get the colostrum - the first secretion of breast which is rich in nutrients. The early feeding of the baby also helps the mother-child bond and the duration of lactation (Cameron, M. and Hofvander, Y. 1983). It was also observed that infants fed early underwent less weight loss and regained their birth weight early with less hypoglycemia (Davis cited by Clavano, N.A. 1982). Therefore, it is important to know when the infant was given the breast for the first time after delivery.

In the present study, it js observed that 64 percent of the traditional and 84 percent of the transitional women were found to start breast feeding the child at any time within the first three days after delivery. The remaining mothers were found to initiate breast feeding only after three days of delivery. This shows that the two groups differ significantly in this aspect (p < 0.05).

Table 4.8 : Initiation of Breast Feeding by Sugali Mothers

Timing of the first breast feeding	Sugali Groups		t-Value
	Tradi-tional	Transi-tional	
Within the first three days after delivery	64 (32)	84 (42)	2.38*
Three days after delivery	36 (18)	16 (8)	2.38*

* p < 0.05

A majority of the traditional and transitional group of women breast fed their children on the first day after birth. This makes it possible for their children to ingest colostrum which is very beneficial to them. The beneficial effects of colostrum are that it provides protection of the baby against infectious diseases (Venkatachalam, P.S. 1982).

The literature reviewed in the earlier chapter reveals that the practice of delayed starting of breast-feeding is prevalent in many rural and urban areas of India. But it is indeed highly satisfying to note that in many tribal communities, the healthy practice of initiating breast feeding from the very first day after delivery is prevalent (Bahl, L. 1979; Mudgal, S. and Rajput, V.S. 1979; Swain, L. 1985; Vimala, V. and Ratnaprabha, C. unpublished).

The tradition of discarding colostrum is rooted since ages and therefore many mothers still avoid the practice of colostrum feeding (Suvarnadevi, P. and Behera, P.L. 1980; Agarwal, 1985). In traditional and transitional Sugali groups, the women breast fed their children three days after delivery reported the colostrum is harmful to infants because it is considered to have remained in the breast for all the nine months of pregnancy. Hence, they are of the opinion that it should not be given to infants. It is alarming to learn that some of the medical staff are still advising the mothers to avoid colostrum, one of the national level studies (Agarwal, 1985) revealed that about 31.5 percent of mothers discarded colostrum on the advice given by nursing staff in Delhi, Haryana, Punjab and Himachal Pradesh. Hence there is a need to increase the awareness of medical staff and other health personal about their role in promoting colostrum feeding practice. Mothers should also be informed about the importance of colostrum in improving health of the infants.

As per the findings of the present study breast feeding is universal among the Sugali mothers. All mothers irrespective of their income and education were found to breast feed infants though there were differences regarding their initiation to breast feeding.

Table 4.9 reveals the non-existence of significant association between income, education of the mother and breast feeding the child at first time.

Prelacteal Feeds

The practice of delaying the commencement of breast feeding for 3 days or for more than 3 days encourages mothers to go for prelacteal feeds. The various kinds of prelacteal feeds used, may affect the infant, if they are prepared and fed in unhygienic way. Moreover when the baby is not put to the breast, during the first 3 days, the stimulus to milk production may be reduced. Also, the baby may not get proper nourishment when it is fed on prelacteal feeds.

Table 4.9 : Initiation of Breast Feeding in Relation to Income of the Family and Education of the Mother

Sl. No.	Income and education levels of the Sugalis	Within the first three days after delivery		Three days after delivery		X^2- Value
		No.	%	No.	%	
1. Traditional						
	Group I	14	73.6	5	26.3	
						1.245
	Group II	18	58.0	13	41.9	
	Illiterate Mothers	30	66.7	15	33.3	
						0.472
	Literate Mothers	2	40.0	3	60.0	
2. Transitional						
	Group I	30	90.0	3	9.0	
						2.094
	Group II	12	70.5	5	29.4	
	Illiterate Mothers	15	88.2	6	35.2	
						2.77
	Literate mothers	27	81.8	2	6.0	

Administration of a variety of prelacteal feeds during the period between birth and initiation of breast feeding can be observed throughout the country. In the present study majority of the traditional and transitional women used honey as prelacteal feed immediately after the child's birth which they believe could satisfy it's hunger. This practice exists among the Santals, a tribe in northern Orissa (Swain, L. 1985). The next popular oral feed includes sugar and glucose water. Few of the respondents used neem oil and castor oil as it is believed that both the oils would remove the toxic substances accumulated in the infant's gastrointestinal system of the past nine months and clean. Neem oil and castro oil have laxative effects and the respondents introduced them to the infant as initial laxatives.

All these factors noted above indicate the need to educate mothers regarding the harmful effects of prelacteal feeds and about the advantages of early initiation of breast feeding.

Breast Feeding

Breast feeding is the natural way of feeding the human infant and is the crucial determinant of growth and survival in the extero-gestate phase. Among the Sugalis of Andhra Pradesh in India some sanctity is attached to the breast milk. They believe that when milk is available with the mother, it is a sin to use the milk of a cow or a buffalo. This is also reported by Lambadis of Andhra Pradesh (Census of India, 1961).

It is found that 98 percent of the traditional and 72 percent of the transitional women have had sufficient breast milk. With regard to output of breast milk, significant difference is seen between traditional and transitional group women (p < 0.05).

Table 4.10 : Traditional and Transitional Sugali Mothers According to Output of Breast Milk

Output of Breast Milk	Sugali Groups		t-Value
	Tradi-tional	Transi-tional	
Insufficient	12 (6)	28 (14)	2.05*
Sufficient	88 (44)	72 (36)	2.05*

* p < 0.05

A larger proportion of the traditional Sugali women than the transitional group have adequate breast milk. The percentage distribution of the Sugali mothers with reference to their output of breast milk, income and education is presented in Table 4.11.

Table 4.11: Distribution of the Traditional and Transitional Sugali Mothers According to the Income of the Family Education of the Mother and the Output of Breast Milk

Output of breast milk	Traditional Sugalis				Transitional Sugalis			
	Group I	Group II	Illite-rates	Lite-rates	Group I	Group II	Illite-rates	Lite-rates
Insufficient	15.7 (3)	9.6 (3)	8.9 (4)	40.0 (2)	24.2 (8)	35.2 (6)	29.4 (15)	27.2 (9)
Sufficient	78.9 (15)	93.5 (29)	91.1 (41)	60.0 (3)	75.7 (25)	64.7 (11)	70.5 (12)	72.7 (24)

In traditional Sugali group, majority of the mothers in Group II (93.5%) and illiterates (91.1%) are found to have sufficient breast milk. In transitional Sugali group, many mothers in Group I (75.7%) and literates (72.7%) are seen with sufficient breast milk.

To increase the supply of their breast milk, half of the traditional Sugali mothers have taken special foods. The items consumed for improving breast feeding performance are chicken, mutton, payasam with rice flour and jaggery, certain greens and vegetables and spices like garlic and coconut. Likewise in the transitional group, 82 percent of the mothers consumed special foods like chicken, mutton, eggs, payasam with rice flour and jaggery, greens and vegetables and spices like garlic and coconut. Table 4.12 shows the percentage distribution of the Sugali mothers according to the types of special foods they consumed to enhance the supply of their breast milk.

Table 4.12 : Type of Special Foods Consumed to Increase the Breast Milk

Special Foods	Sugali Mothers	
	Traditional	*Transitional*
Chicken	32 (16)	74 (37)
Meat	6 (3)	56 (28)
Eggs	--	28 (14)
Payasam	50 (25)	62 (31)
Greens and vegetables	32 (16)	28 (14)
Spices	22 (11)	16 (8)

The above table shows that more Sugali mothers in the transitional group are found to consume special foods except Greens and vegetables and spices than those in the traditional group.

The chi-square value in Table 4.13 indicates that the use of special foods for increasing breast milk has no relation either to the income or educational levels of the two groups of Sugalis studied.

Table 13 : Traditional and Transitional Sugali Mothers According to Their Income of the Family, Education of the Mother and Special Foods Consumed to Increase Quantity of Their Breast Milk

Sl. No.	Levels of Income and Literacy	Special Foods taken		Special Foods not taken		X^2- Value
		No.	%	No.	%	
1.	**Traditional**					
	Group I	10	52.6	9	47.3	
						0.084
	Group II	15	48.3	16	51.6	
	Illiterate Mothers	22	48.9	23	51.1	

	Literate Mothers	3	60.0	2	40.0	
2.	**Transitional**					
	Group I	30	90.9	3	9.0	
						3.59
	Group II	11	64.7	6	35.2	
	Illiterate Mothers	13	76.4	4	23.5	
						0.115
	Literate mothers	28	84.8	5	15.1	

While discussing the breast feeding practice, duration of exclusive breast feeding and total duration of breast feeding are the two important factors to be considered with regard to infant nutrition. It is well established that breast feeding for prolonged duration is more beneficial for the health of the infants. At the same time prolonged breast feeding without additional supplements after the age of 6 months is detrimental to the health of the baby.

When the duration of breast feeding (Table 4.14) is taken into consideration it is noticed that 22 percent of the traditional mothers as against 58 percent of transitional mothers breast fed their children for 6 months to one year. This shows a highly significant difference (p<0.01) between the two groups of mothers. Fifty eight per cent and 42 percent of the mothers in the traditional and transitional groups respectively breast fed their children 1 year to 2 years. This shows no significant difference between them. Only 20 percent of the traditional mothers gave breast milk to their children for more than 2 years. None of the mothers in transitional group did so.

Table 4.14 : Duration of Breast Feeding

Duration of Breast Feeding	Sugali Groups		t-Value
	Tradi-tional	Transi-tional	
6 months – 1 year	22 (11)	58 (29)	4.0**
1 year – 2 years	58 (29)	42 (21)	1.64
Above 2 years	20 (10)	--	--

** p < 0.01

The proportion of the mothers with regard to duration of breast feeding in the traditional and transitional groups are shown clearly in relation to income level and education of the mother (Table 4.15). Among the traditional group, irrespective of income and education, a majority of them breast fed their children for one to two years. Whereas in transitional group only half of the mothers breast fed their children for one to two years. In traditional group, some (32.2% of Group II, 13.3% of illiterates) of the mothers found to breast fed their child beyond 2 years. In transitional group none of them are found to breast feed beyond two years. In this group, a majority of the (Group I and literates mothers found to breast fed their children for 6 months to one year.

Table 4.15: Duration of Breast Feeding in Relation to Income of the Family and Education of the Mother

Duration of Breast feeding	Sugali Mothers							
	Traditional Sugalis				Transitional Sugalis			
	Group I	Group II	Illite-rates	Lite-rates	Group I	Group II	Illite-rates	Lite-rates
6 months – 1 year	31.5 (6)	16.1 (5)	22.2 (10)	20.0 (1)	66.7 (22)	41.1 (7)	47.0 (8)	63.6 (21)
1 year – 2 years	68.4 (13)	51.6 (16)	64.4 (29)	80.0 (4)	30.3 (11)	58.8 (10)	52.9 (9)	36.3 (12)
Above 2 Years	--	32.2 (10)	13.3 (6)	--	--	--	--	--

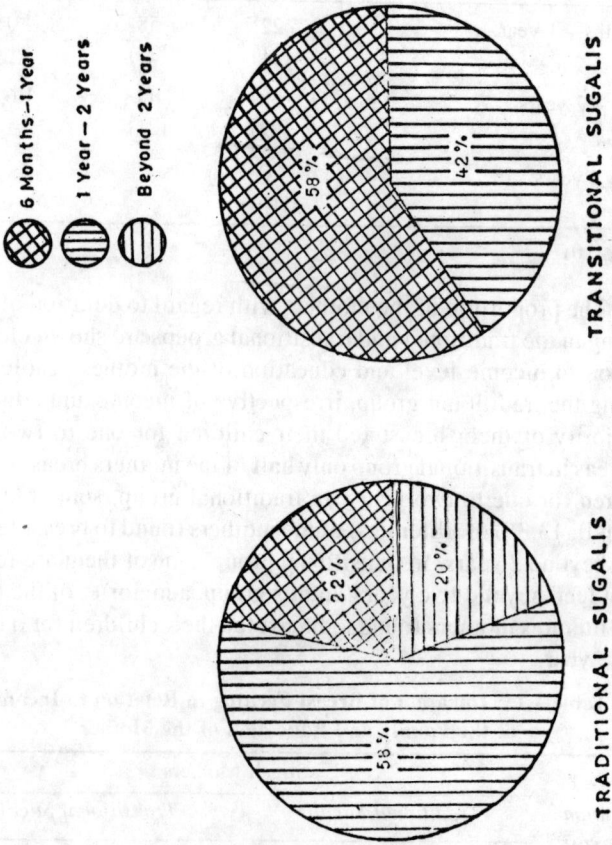

6 Months–1 Year

1 Year – 2 Years

Beyond 2 Years

58 %

42 %

TRANSITIONAL SUGALIS

22 %

20 %

58 %

TRADITIONAL SUGALIS

Fig. 1 : Duration of Breast Feeding

In review of literature the studies by various researchers like Dube, L. (1949), Belavady, B. et al (1959), Sampath, R. (1964), Bahl, L. (1979), Mudgal, S. and Rajput, V.S. (1979), Swain, L. (1985), Das, K. and Ghosh, A.K. (1985) and Rizvi, S.N.H. (1985) found out the practice of prolonged breast feeding among different tribal communities. In the present study also majority of the traditional group Sugalis have this practice.

The mother in both the groups expressed that if the child is not crying and playing happily then the baby is satisfied with breast milk. If the mother has excess of milk then she removes it and pours it on the wall of the house or plants.

Substitutes for Breast Milk

When the breast milk is inadequate or completely not available (12% traditional and 28% transitional Sugali mothers) the provision of substitute milk is presented. Among the children of the traditional Sugali group, cow's milk and goat's milk was found to have been supplied to 8% and 4% respectively. Among the children of the transitional Sugali group, 16 percent, 8 percent and 4 percent received cow's milk, goat milk and milk powder respectively. Table 4.16 shows that majority of Group I mothers of the traditional group and Group II mothers of the transitional group are found to give cow's and goat's milk to their children. Irrespective of education, the traditional and transitional mothers offered cow's and goat's milk to their children. Only in transitional Sugali group, Group I and literate mothers offered commercial preparations.

Table 4.16 : Breast Milk Substitutes Used

Type of Milk other than breast milk offered to the child	Traditional Sugalis				Transitional Sugalis			
	Group I	Group II	Illite-rates	Lite-rates	Group I	Group II	Illite-rates	Lite-rates
Cows Milk	10.5	6.4	8.9	---	12.1	23.5	41.1	30.0
	(2)	(2)	(4)		(4)	(4)	(7)	(1)
Goat Milk	5.2	3.2	--	40.0	6.0	11.7	5.8	9.0
	(1)	(1)		(2)	(2)	(2)	(1)	(3)
Commercial preparations	--	--	--	--	0.6	--	--	6.0
					(2)			(2)

Out of the 6 traditional Sugali mothers who introduced substitute milks to their children, 4 mothers introduced the milk after the first year of child's life and 2 mothers introduced the milk before the first year of child's life. The milk is given to the children in a tumbler. In some cases, they improvise feeding bottle using an old tonic bottle.

Out of 14 mothers in the transitional group of mothers who introduced substitute milk to their children, 6 mothers introduced the milk after the first year of child's life and the remaining 8 mothers introduced the milk before the first year of child's life. They offer milk in old tonic bottles or tumblers.

On the whole the first preference is given to cow's milk and next to goat's milk in both the Sugali groups. Very few transitional Sugali mothers used milk powder.

Supplementary Feeding

The age of introduction of supplementary feeding in the children of the traditional and transitional Sugali mothers varied from three months to eighteen months. None of the mothers among the traditional Sugalis introduced supplementary feeding before 6 months. A few mothers (16%) introduced supplemtary feeding at 7-12 months. Majority of the mothers (84%) among the traditional Sugalis introduced supplemtary feeding between one year to one and half-a-year.

As far as the transitional Sugalis concerned it is noticed that 18 percent of the mothers started giving supplementary food to their children before they reached 6 months of age. Sixty percent of them introduced their children to supplemtary feeding when they reached 7-12 months and 22 percent are started giving supplemtary foods to their children at the age of one year or one and half-a-year.

On the whole more number of traditional Sugali mothers (84%) delayed supplementary feeding their children. The percentage of such women (16%) is smaller among the traditional Sugalis. Many mothers (60%) in the transition group of Sugalis started giving supplementary foods at 7-12 months age. There is significant difference (p<0.01) between these two Sugali groups with regard to their children's age at which they introduce supplementary foods to them (Table 4.17).

Many people, because of ignorance or traditional beliefs delayed introducing supplementary food to their infants. In several

Table 4.17 : Age at which Supplementary Feeding is Introduced

Age of the children at the time when they are given supplementary foods	Traditional	Transitional	t-value
Before 6 months	--	18 (9)	--
7–12 months	16 (8)	60 (30)	5.11**
1.1 – 1.5 years	84 (42)	22 (11)	7.12**

** p < 0.01

instances in the traditional group it was observed that solid food is introduced to children only around 12th or 18th month of age or later, because of the belief that as long as baby is breast fed there is no need of any other type of food. Venkatachalam, P.S. and Rebello, L.M. (1966) findings also supported the same notion.

Studies on lactation performance of Indian nursing women by NIN revealed that upto 6 months after delivery there is generally a steady rise in the output of milk, Subsequently the milk output diminishes. If the baby is to maintain the expected rate of growth and remain healthy and well nourished, supplementary feeding has to be resorted to at about the six months of life.

The supplementary foods used by the mothers by the traditional Sugalis are Sangati, plain boiled rice or rice with rasam, idly, banana, guava fruit. On the other hand the mothers in the transitional Sugali group used rice with dhal and rasam, idly, biscuit, egg, banana and other fruits.

There is association between income, education of the mother and the age of the children at which the supplementary foods are introduced. This is shown in Table 4.18. In the traditional group, income (p < 0.01) and education of the mother (p < 0.05) are associated with the age of child at which the supplementary foods given. Greater percentage of Group II income families and illiterate mothers are seen with introducing the supplementary foods later age (during 1.1 to 1.5 years) when compared to Group I and literate mothers. In the transitional group no association is found with regard to the income of the mothers and the age of the child at which the supplementary foods

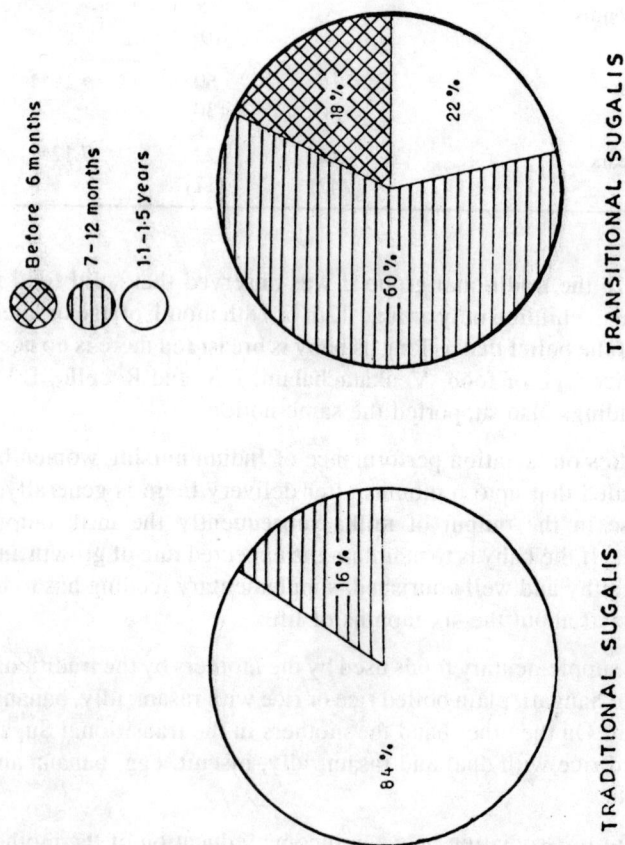

Fig. 2 : Age at which Supplementary Feeding is Introduced

given. But there is correspondence between education of the mother and the age of the child at which the supplementary foods given ($p<0.01$) i.e., literate mothers are found to seen with introducing the supplementary foods at early age (before 6 months, 7-12 months).

Table 4.18 : Age of Introduction of Supplementary Feeding in Relation to Income of the Family and Education of the Mother

Sl. No.	Sugalis	Before 6 months		7–12 Months		1.1–1.5 years		X^2 – value
		No.	%	No.	%	No.	%	
1. Traditional								
	Group I	--	--	37	36.8	12	63.0	7.54**
	Group II	--	--	1	3.2	30	96.7	
	Illiterate mothers	--	--	5	11.1	40	88.8	4.77*
	Literate Mothers	--	--	3	60.0	2	40.0	
2. Transitional								
	Group I	6	18.1	21	63.1	6	18.1	0.55
	Group II	3	17.6	9	52.9	5	29.4	
	Illiterate Mothers	--	--	8	47.0	9	52.9	11.75**
	Literate Mothers	9	27.2	22	66.7	2	6.0	

* p<0.05
** p <0.01

Weaning Practices

The term weaning can be separated into two primary usages. The first sense of the term refers to the gradual process of removing the child from the breast and dependence on breast milk. The second sense of the term refers to the process of introducing solid foods into the infant's diet. The Sugali children are weaned by the age of 2½ years with no special efforts by the mothers. They are weaned either gradually or abruptly on account of next pregnancy, insufficient milk, or by the provision of substantial solid diet, or due to mothers leaving for outstation work. When the mothers find it difficult to wean a child,

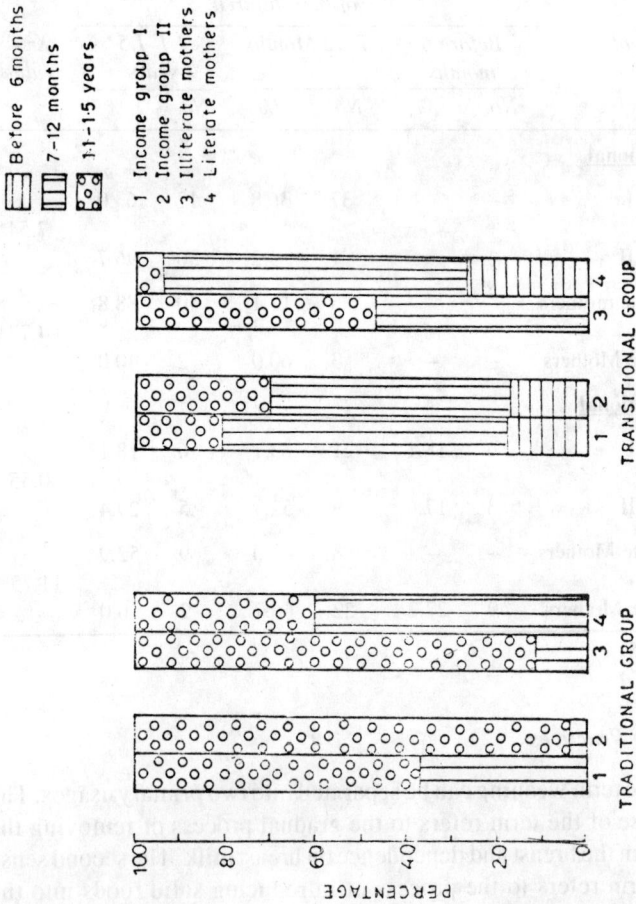

Fig. 3 : Age of Introduction of Supplementary Feeding in Relation to Income and Education of the Mother

they resort to various methods such as applying of bitter substances like the paste of neem leaves to the breast; offering of various foods to children or tying of jasmine flowers to the breast to dry the milk. Another method is to eat Brinjal, drumstick leaves and roasted bengal gram as they would 'dry up' the milk in the breast. Still another method to dry up the milk is to wrap up a dry cloth tightly cover the breasts.

For nutritional reasons, the introduction of semisolid/solid foods to a wholly or partially breast fed infant may become necessary between the fourth and sixth month. At this age breast milk or top milk alone may not satisfy the infant's needs.

According to Woodruff (1978) the introduction of semisolid foods should be determined by developmental readiness for semisolid food and the ability to respond to a spoon by recognition and the ability of the tongue and swallowing mechanism to deal with non-liquid food. This developmental stage occurs between 3 to 6 months of age in most of the infants. Studies have proved that early weaning before 3 months or even late weaning are not advisable. As early weaning generally causes weaning diarrhoea and late introduction of solids after 6 months often leads to undernutrition in infants. (Wyon, J.B. and Gordon, J.E. 1971, Waterlow, J.L. and Thomson, A.M. 1979, Waterlow, J.L. 1981 and NIN Annual Report 1982).

In the traditional Sugalis, children from the age of 2½ years are red on the usual diet prepared for the family. However this diet is given to them in a mashed form. No special food is prepared for the child. The children in the transitional Sugali group receive usual foods at an early age when compared to those in the traditional Sugali group. In the traditional group the child usually shows interest in food and takes initiative in picking up food and eating. The mother and elder children in the family allow the child to eat by itself but they do not feed the child with their own hands. The feeding sessions are unsupervised. On the contrary, in the transitional Sugali group the mother or elder children in the family serves food to child with their own hands and pay attention to some extent.

After 2 years of age, very few families with high income (Group I) in the traditional group provided some chocolates biscuits or other sweets to the children. In the transitional group also more number of families with higher income (Group I) feed the children with such energy foods.

As the educational status and income of the parents increases the supplementary feeding pattern of the infants also increases in quality as well as in quantity (Maidya, et al 1970).

Health and Hygienic Practices

Physical well-being is an important component of total health. The foundation for health and hygiene are laid in early childhood. Good personal hygiene is very important to maintain good health.

Common Ailments in Children

Physical health condition of the children is a major factor that concerns all parents. Hurlock, E.B. (1978) said that if the children are healthy, their performance will be good in all aspects of development. In the present study the Sugali children are often found to suffer from cold, cough, fever, diarrhoea, scabies and measles (Table 4.19). Cold and cough are simple but persistent problems. Fourty-six percent of children in the traditional group and 40 percent of the children in the transitional group were found to suffer from cold. There is no significant difference between these two groups with regard to cold problem. Fifty six percent of the traditional and 34 percent of the transitional Sugali children suffered from cough. The statistical difference between these groups is significant ($p < 0.05$). Fourty six percent of the children in both the groups suffered from fever. Diarrhoes is very common, 64 percent of the children in the traditional and 38 percent of the children in the transitional group suffered from diarrhoes. It shows a significant difference ($p < 0.01$) between traditional and transitional groups with regard to diarrhoeal problem. More of the children (54%) in the traditional group suffered from scabies than those (30%) in the transitional group. This also shows significant difference ($p<0.05$). All rashes on the face and body other than prickly heat are termed as 'pox'. It may be small pox, chicken pox or measles. In the present study, only in traditional group, 6 percent of the children suffered from measles.

From the above findings, it is observed that fever is found to be seen in nearly half of the children of the traditional and transitional groups. A greater proportion of children in traditional group are found to suffer from cold, cough, diarrhoea, scabies, Measles when compared to children in transitional group. The reason may be that the traditional mothers are not taking adequate care about environmental sanitation and personal hygiene of their children due to economic constraints, poor living facilities and a lack of awareness.

Table 4.19 : Common Ailments in Children

Name of the Disease	Sugali Children		t-Value
	Tradi-tional	Transi-tional	
Cold	46 (23)	40 (20)	0.61
Cough	56 (28)	34 (17)	2.29*
Fever	46 (23)	46 (23)	--
Diarrhoea	64 (32)	38 (19)	2.70**
Scabies	54 (27)	30 (15)	2.52**
Measles	6 (3)	--	--

* $p < 0.05$;   ** $p < 0.01$

Table 4.20 shows the many children in the income Group II families of the traditional group suffered from cold, cough and fever. Diarrhoea, scabies were mostly seen in income Group I traditional families. In income Group II families of the transitional group majority of the children suffered from cold and cough. More children in income Group I families of the transitional group suffered from fever. Diarrhoea and scabies mostly occurred in income Group II families of transitional group.

Type of Treatment Given to Children

Generally speaking, tribal societies are simple, isolated and remain deprived of the modern medical services. But diseases occur in all societies, irrespective of the level of development, and each society makes certain provisions for understanding the occurrence of illness and for coping with it. The therapeutical practices of a society are the set of beliefs regarding the ways in which illness can be cured and prevented.

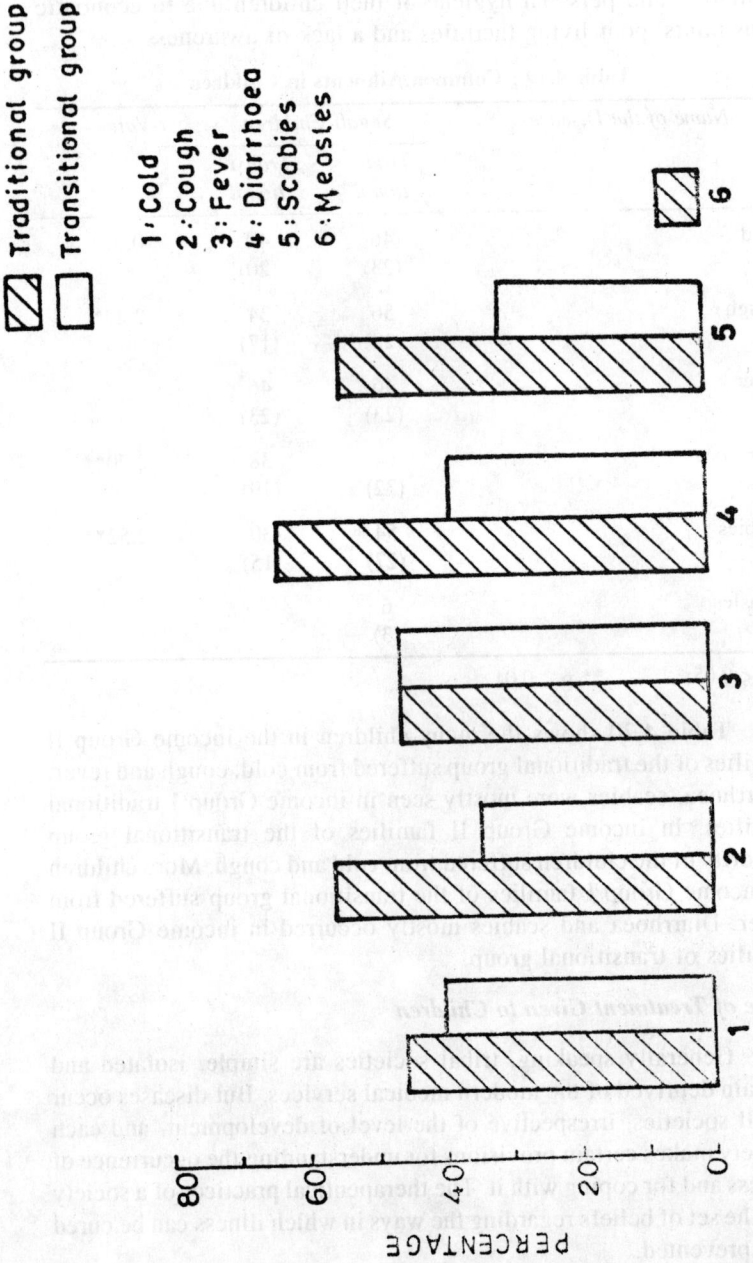

Fig. 4 : Common Ailments in Children

Traditional group

Transitional group

1: Cold
2: Cough
3: Fever
4: Diarrhoea
5: Scabies
6: Measles

**Table 4.20 : Common Ailments in Children in Relation
to Income of the Family**

Name of the disease	Traditional Group		Transitional Group	
	Group I	Group II	Group I	Group II
Cold	36.8 (7)	51.6 (16)	30.3 (10)	58.8 (10)
Cough	52.6 (10)	58.0 (18)	24.2 (8)	52.9 (9)
Fever	36.8 (7)	51.6 (16)	54.5 (18)	29.4 (5)
Diarrhoea	89.4 (17)	48.3 (15)	33.3 (11)	47.0 (8)
Scabies	78.9 (15)	38.7 (12)	27.2 (9)	35.2 (6)
Measles	5.2 (1)	6.4 (2)	--	--

Table 4.21 shows the children in the traditional and transitional
sample families who were given indigenous, magical and allopathic
treatment in times of illness, It is evident that majority of the children
in the traditional group are given indigenous (64%) and magical (22%)
rather than allopathic treatment (14%) because most of the parents still
hold their traditional cultural beliefs and practices, could not afford
to give medical aid to their children and due to inaccessibility of health
centres. On the other hand, in the transitional group, though they too
provide indigenous (50%) and magical treatment (12%), they also use
allopathic treatment (38%). There is significant difference ($p<0.01$)
statistically with regard to using the allopathic treatment in the
traditional and transitional groups.

Table 4.21 : Type of Treatment Given to the Children

Type of Treatment	Sugali Children		t-Value
	Tradi-tional	Transi-tional	
Indigenous	64 (32)	50 (25)	1.49
Magical	22 (11)	12 (6)	1.35
Allopathic	14 (7)	38 (19)	2.85**

** $p < 0.01$

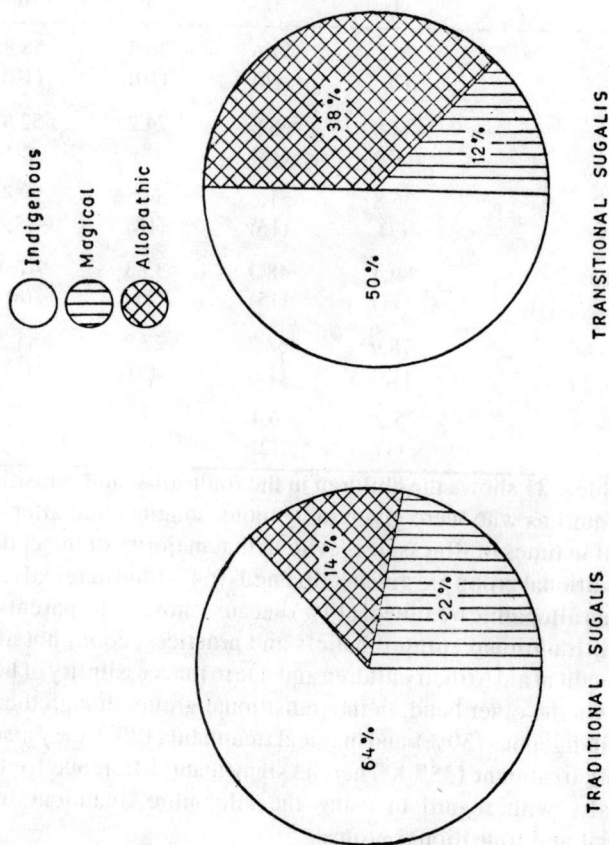

Fig. 5 : Type of Treatment Given to the Children

When Sugali children suffer from cold and cough their parents usually do not take them to the doctor. Instead they use a variety of indigenous treatments. The herbs used in the preparation of indigenous treatments are Kukkathulasi (occimum basilicus), Kapparillaku (coleus aromaticus), Tamalapaku (piper betel), Jajikaya (myristics fragrans), Tummi (leuces aspara). These are used in combination with turmeric, milk Guntagingaraku (Eclipa alba), Karakkaya (Termivalia chebula).

All the above mentioned herbal preparations are used for cold and cough. If the cold and cough continues then pepper, clove, ginger, garlic and betel leaves are boiled in water and a teaspoon of this essence is given to the baby three times a day for three days. If the cough becomes persistent it is suspected to be whooping cough. The treatment for this is to tie and yellow thread interwoven with fruits of Kanuga (pongamiagalbra) around the neck of child, Further they customarily give meat of deer to children during whooping cough. Earlier Hemalatha Rani (1980) also found that the above type of treatment was given to cure whooping cough in children of low class families of two villages in Chittoor district. They also treat with the roots of Vippa (pachygone ovata).

The Sugalis believe that fever is due to fear of darkness or animals or due to evil eye (dishti). Parents give the magical treatment of tying of nallatadu (black thread) blessed by a priest or an elder member of the community on the child's wrist and the waist. However, some Sugali mothers in the traditional and transitional group cure fever by accepting medicines from the village health worker during her visits to the village. If fever becomes serious then the child is taken to a doctor.

Diarrhoea is very common among the children in traditional sample families. However only a few families provide treatment for diarrhoea due to ignorance and poverty. Further these people do not consider this as a disease at all.

Generally, the magical treatment like tying a thread by magician is given for diarrhoea. If diarrhoes persists for a number of days in a serious state, then only they provide allopathic treatment to their children in both traditional and transitional groups.

For curing scabies the Sugalis generally use sulphur powder mixed with water.

Generally mothers do not opt for allopathic treatment for measles because of their belief that it is a visitation of the mother-goddess (Ammavaru) and that she would get angry if they use medicines and the condition will worsen. No bath is given to the child till the 9th day and turmeric powder mixed in plain water, will be sprinkled in the room and neam leaves will be kept at the side of the child's head. During these 9 days the family members do not visit any other family.

Thus it is noticed that the type of treatment given for common diseases varies. For some diseases like cold and cough, indigenous treatment is very much preferred. Indigenous treatment includes the application of home remedies prepared from herbal ingredients. The women folk in both traditional and transitional groups have extensive knowledge of home remedies to cure common ailments like cold, cough etc.

The practices of magical treatment are practiced from time immemorial. In earlier days, as the medical science had not developed in ancient and medieval periods these practices were widely practiced. They had taken deep roots in the life of the people and continue to exercise their influence on the villages. Many believe in magical treatment and they are convinced that it works. Magic has its psychological effects on the people. Traditional and transitional Sugalis have strong faith in magical treatment and practice it. Dave, P., Hakim, M, and Tavkar, N (1984), Dash, J. (1985) conducted studies on tribals and found that the concept and treatment of the diseases were very much associated with the magico-religious beliefs.

In the event of taking allopathic treatment, majority of the parents in the traditional (88%) and transitional group (64%) take their children to a Government hospital and the rest 12 percent in traditional and 36 percent in transitional group take their children to a private hospital.

A majority of the Sugali parents from traditional and transitional groups take allopathic treatment at government hospitals due to their low income and the others take it at private nursing homes. The reasons given for resorting to private hospital treatment were that they were located at far places, the services rendered were poor, they had to waste a long-time waiting for their turn and the harsh treatment by the doctors and other staff at the Government hospital.

On the whole, the indigenous and magical treatment is very much prevalent in the traditional group than transitional group due to their beliefs and practices. But among non-tribals also the belief in indigenous and magical treatment is strong and practice it. (Minturn, L. and Hitchcock, J.T. (1964(, Madhavi, J. (1979), Hemalatha Rani, P. (1980), Sobhavathi, J. (1980), Nagabhushanamma, K. (1984). In relation to allopathic treatment the number is increased from traditional to transitional group due to urbanization and education.

In the traditional and transitional groups no significant association is seen between income, education of the mother, age of the child and type of treatment given to children (Table 4.22).

Table 22 : Type of Treatment Given to Children in Relation to Income of the Family, Education of the Mother and Age of the Child

Sl. No.	Income, Education of the mother and age of the child	Type of Treatment						X^2 – value
		Indigenous		Magical		Allopathic		
		No.	%	No.	%	No.	%	
1. Traditional								
	Group I	11	57.89	4	21.0	4	21.0	
								0.522
	Group II	21	67.70	7	22.5	3	9.67	
	Illiterate mothers	31	68.90	9	20.0	5	11.10	
								2.1806
	Literate Mothers	1	20.0	2	40.0	2	40.00	
	0–1 year age	8	53.3	4	26.7	3	20.0	
	1–3 years age	10	58.8	5	29.4	2	11.7	1.2601
	3–5 years age	14	77.8	2	11.1	2	11.1	
2. Transitional								
	Group I	18	54.5	3	9.0	12	36.3	
								0.3301
	Group II	7	41.1	3	17.6	7	41.1	
	Illiterate Mothers	10	58.8	4	23.5	3	17.6	
								3.812
	Literate Mothers	15	45.4	4	23.5	3	17.6	
	0–1 year age	12	54.5	3	13.6	7	31.8	
								1.8692
	1–3 years age	7	43.7	2	12.5	7	43.7	
	3–5 years age	6	50.0	1	8.3	5	41.7	

Besides taking recourse to magical, indigenous, allopathic treatment, people use several incantations or make vows to the gods to cure or prevent illness of their children. The replies to the questions on this subject reveal that almost all the sample families are found to use incantations or made vows to the gods for an easy or speedy recovery of children from illnesses. The vows are fulfilled after the children recover from illness.

When the child falls ill without any apparent reason it's mother thinks that some one in the neighbourhood might have cast an evil eye on the child. The evil-eye is considered as a source of great danger to children. It is cast on the child by someone who is jealous of the child. All babies are protected against it by a black dot put on the chin or foot during the first few weeks of life or on occasions for several years. Mothers of handsome children are warned that they should not enrobe the children well and make them look pretty, one must never praise a child by saying that it is pretty or exceptionally big and healthy, such praise may bring bad luck to the child and leave the praises open to the suspicion of throwing an evil-eye.

Hundred percent of the families in the traditional Sugali group and 94 percent of the families in the transitional group believe evil-eye (dishti). The victims of evil eye are the children aged between 0-1 year. To ward off the effects of the evil-eye, the elders or mother take a few red chillies, fallen hair and some salt crystals into the left hand then rotate their hand first in the clock-wise and then in anti-clock-wise direction while muttering some incantations and finally throw them into the fire. It is a belief that if the child is taken possession of by evil-eyes, these items when thrown in the fire would emit a bad smell otherwise not. Some of the women treat evil eye with broom stick, stone and camphor.

Twelve Sugali families in the traditional group and 7 families in the transitional group have taken vows to cure the illness of their children. Most of the families in both the groups have no money to spare for such practices though they did believe in them. As every Sugali family has ancestor and clan deities to worship they make offerings and sacrifices to them when there is any sickness in the family. Ramachandra Reddy, M. (1984) reported that the Sugalis worship Hindu pantheon besides the local deities Tulasamma, Mallamma, Maremma, Ankalamma, Reddemma, Poleramma, Maisemma to cure from measles and other diseases.

The same practice exists among the non-tribal communities also Aphale, C. (1976) found that a larger proportion of intermediate and Scheduled caste families practiced both the 'Dishti' and 'vows' to cure or prevent illness in children.

All the families (100%) in the traditional group and 78 percent of the families in the transitional group believe in evil-spirits. They take the help of magician (siana) to know the cause of the child's sickness and cure the disease caused by the evil-spirits.

In the traditional and transitional Sugali groups, the dietary treatment also prevalent during sickness of the children. The Sugali mothers avoid certain foods depending upon the nature of the sickness. They avoid foods like berries, raw tamarind fruit, sweet lime, green gram and tomato when they suffer from cold and cough because these are considered as foods that cool the body system and their effect will be serious if they are consumed during cold and cough. 'Hot foods' like jaggery, eggs, bengal gram, bajra, papaya etc. are avoided during fevers. Most of the mothers stated that the child should not be given rice during fever since they believe that a sick child cannot digest rice properly. 'Cold foods', banana fruit, dhal, vegetables, excess water to the child are avoided during diarrhoea. During measles heat producing foods are avoided.

The foregoing discussion shows that mothers in traditional and transitional group practice dietary treatment to the children. To get knowledge in this aspect appropriate nutrition and health education is necessary for both the groups. Hygienic manner of feeding the child has to be encouraged.

Immunization Practices

Most of the infectious diseases, which either retard the child's growth or cause handicaps or sometimes lead to death, can be prevented by immunization. Therefore, immunization against child-hood diseases is an important issue for better growth and survival of infants.

Table 4.23 reveals that in traditional Sugali group, 56 percent of the children are immunized against diseases like Polio, D.P.T. and measles. Eighty two percent of the children in the transitional group immunized against disease like B.C.G., polio, D.P.T. and measles.

This shows high significant difference (p<0.01) between traditional and transitional groups with regard to immunization given to children.

Table 4.23 : Immunization Practices

Particulars	Sugali Children		t-Value
	Tradi-tional	Transi-tional	
Immunized	56	82	2.95**
	(28)	(41)	
Not Immunized	44	18	2.95**
	(22)	(9)	

** p < 0.01

In the traditional Sugali group, a majority of the children (90%) have received immunization from village health worker. In the transitional group, some of the children (36%) have received immunization through Government hospital.

From the above data, it is observed that in the traditional families, the immunization status of the children is unsatisfactory when compared to the children in transitional families. This may be due to lack of awareness and large family size (more than 3 children). Dabi, D.R., Sinha, R. N. and Gupta, B.D. (1983) reported that reduction in family size may improve the immunization status of the undergives by improving the socio-economic status of the community.

Only in the transitional group, B.C.G. vaccination is given to the children. Vijay's, H. et al (1976) study revealed that educational status of the mothers is correlated with B.C.G. vaccination given to the children and the educational status of the parents is positively related to the overall immunization status of children.

Table 4.24 reveals that a higher percentage of income Group I families, literate mothers in both traditional and transitional groups get their children immunized. Vijay, H., Ghosh, S. et al (1976) reported that better economic and educational status of mothers lead to increased acceptance of all immunizations. The chi-square values indicates (Table 4.24) no significant association between income, education of the mother and immunization given to the children. Since immunization is provided free of charge there is no relation between economic status and immunization.

Table 4.24 : **Immunization Practices to the Children According to the Income of the Family and Literacy Levels of Mothers**

Sl. No.	Income and Literacy Levels of mothers	Sugali Children				X^2 – Value
		Immunized No.	%	Not Immunized No.	%	
1.	**Traditional**					
	Group I	12	63.1	7	36.8	
						0.253
	Group II	16	51.6	15	48.3	
	Illiterate Mothers	24	53.3	21	46.7	
						0.44
	Literate Mothers	27	80.0	1	20.0	
2.	**Transitional**					
	Group I	27	81.8	6	18.1	
						0.1166
	Group II	14	82.3	3	17.6	
	Illiterate Mothers	11	64.7	6	35.2	
						3.59
	Literate Mothers	30	40.9	3	9.1	

Immunising every child against all the communicable diseases is of public health importance and is a basic need of the child and community. This indicates the need for health education among Sugalis of traditional group to create awareness and to utilize the existing health services maximally.

Cleaning of Teeth by Children

Personal hygiene includes all those personal factors which influence the health and well-being of an individual. It comprises many day-to-day activities such as care of body related to cleaning the teeth, bathing and care of clothes etc. Personal hygiene affects primarily the health of the individual and is largely connected with the standard of living (Park and Park, 1980).

In the present study, it is observed that 18 percent of the children in the traditional group started cleaning their teeth after 4-5 years. But in the transitional group the corresponding proportion is 58% and the children started to clean their teeth before 3 years. Almost 82 percent of the children in the traditional group and 42 percent of the children in the transitional groups had not yet started to clean their teeth even by 5 years. The difference between the traditional and the transitional groups with regard to cleaning the teeth is significant (p < 0.01).

When the traditional mothers asked about their attitudes towards cleaning of children's teeth is that they believe as their children grow older, they will learn by themselves (Narayan's, S. (1983) study on Oraon tribe revealed that children did not clean their teeth upto the age of eight years). Whereas in the transitional group, the mothers are encouraging from early years and also do most of their cleaning when they are too young with the result more than half of the transitional children started to clean their teeth before 3 years.

In the traditional group, a majority of the children had not regularly cleaned their teeth compared to the transitional group due to indifference of mothers. No association exists between income, education of the mother and cleaning of teeth by children in the traditional group. In the transitional group also no relationship is found between income and cleaning of teeth by children. When education level of the mother increases, the cleaning of teeth by children also increases (p < 0.01) in the transitional group,

Nearly 80 percent of the children in the traditional group and 40 percent of the children in the transitional group use ash, charcoal powder, salt, snuff, brick-powder, neem twig, banyan twig etc. to clean their teeth. The remaining 20 percent in the traditional group use cheap tooth powder as cleaning agent. In the transitional group, 20 percent of the children are found to use cheap tooth powder and the rest use tooth brush and powder/paste as cleansing agent. Due to rise in income and urbanisation, the children in transitional group are found to use costly tooth powder/ paste and brush whereas in traditional group, more of them are found to use the same.

Frequency of Bath

Table 4.25 shows that 20 percent of the children in the traditional 44 percent of the children in the transitional group receive body bath twice a day (It shows significant difference, p < 0.01). Fourteen percent in the traditional group and 24 percent in the transitional group receive body bath daily in the morning. Thirty percent in the traditional group and 32 percent in the transitional group receive body-bath once in three days. Only in the traditional group, 36 percent receive body-bath once in a week.

Table 4.25 : Frequency of Bath Given to Children

Sl. No.	Particulars	Sugali Children		t–Value
		Traditional	Transitional	
1.	**Body Bath**			
	Twice in a day	20 (10)	44 (22)	2.7**
	Once in a day	14 (7)	24 (12)	1.29
	Once in three days	30 (15)	32 (16)	--
	Once in a Week	36 (18)	--	--
2.	**Head Bath**			
	Once in two days	16 (8)	36 (18)	2.38*
	Once in 4 days	6 (3)	14 (7)	3.96**
	Once in a Week	22 (11)	38 (19)	1.80
	Once in 15 days	38 (19)	12 (6)	4.4**
	Once in a month	18 (9)	--	--

** $p < 0.01$;　　* $p < 0.05$

Regarding head bath of the children, 16 percent in the traditional and 36 percent in the transitional group receive head bath once in two days (It shows significant difference $p<0.05$) 6 percent in the traditional group and 14 percent in the transitional group receive head bath once in 4 days (It also shows significant difference, $p<0.01$), 22 percent in the traditional group and 38 percent in the transitional group receive head bath one in a week. Thirty eight percent in the traditional group and 12 percent in the transitional group receive head bath once in fifteen days (It is significantly different at 0.01 percent level) and only in the traditional group, 18 percent receive head bath once in a month.

In the traditional and transitional groups as the education of the mother and income decreases the children were found to have bath less frequently and vice-versa. When age of the child increases, they were found to have bath less frequently. (refer Table 4.26)

Table 4.26 : Frequency of Body Bath Given to the Children in Relation to Income of the Family and Literacy of Mothers

Sl. No.	Income and Literacy Levels of Sugali mothers	Frequency of Body bath given to children							
		Once in a Day		2 Times a Day		Once in 2 Days		Once in a Week	
		No.	%	No.	%	No.	%	No.	%
1.	**Traditional**								
	Group I	2	10.5	4	21.0	8	42.1	5	26.3
	Group II	5	16.1	6	19.3	7	22.5	18	41.9
	Illiterate Mothers	6	13.3	9	20.0	14	31.1	16	84.2
	Literate Mothers	1	20.0	1	20.0	1	20.0	2	6.45
	0–1 year age child	5	33.0	10	66.7	--	--	--	--
	1–3 years age child	2	13.3	--	--	15	88.2	--	--
	3–5 years age child	--	--	--	--	--	--	15	83.3
2.	**Transitional**								
	Group I	8	24.2	16	48.4	9	27.2	--	--
	Group II	4	23.5	6	35.2	7	41.1	--	--
	Illiterate Mothers	2	11.7	3	17.6	12	70.5	--	--
	Literate Mothers	10	30.3	19	57.5	4	12.1	--	--
	0–1 year age child	--	--	22	100.0	--	--	--	--
	1–3 years age child	9	37.5	--	--	7	43.7	--	--
	3–5 years age child	3	25.0	--	--	9	75.0	--	--

As the income increases, the children were found to have head bath more frequently in the traditional group. In the transitional group, when income and education of the mother increases the frequency of head bath given to children also increases. It also shows that when age of the child increases the frequency of head bath given also decreases in both the groups. (refer Table 4.27).

From the above findings it is observed that on the whole the attention given to personal hygiene of the children with regard to cleaning of teeth, bathing given is seen to be poor in the traditional group when compared to children in the transitional group. The mothers in transitional group seem to be aware of the importance of personal hygiene for maintaining sound physical and mental health of the children. It may be because most of them belong to the higher economic status group with better education.

The preceding discussion shows that there is a need to educate the mothers specially who are belonging to traditional group about the importance of personal hygiene.

The percentage distribution of Sugali children according to the accessories used for their bath. All the transitional Sugali families use hot water for bathing their children but 10 percent of the Sugali families in the traditional group use cold water for bath. (Significant difference at 0.05 percent level). More than half of the families in transitional group use soap nut (Sikay) powder for head bath (significant difference, $p < 0.01$), while corresponding proportion of those in the traditional group is only 16 percent. In the traditional group, detergent soaps are mostly used for washing the head of the children (significant difference at 0.01 percent level). Again in the transitional group, many families use turmeric powder, oil and sunnipindi as materials to clean the body during head bath. While in the traditional group, bath or detergent soaps are used for the purpose. (significant difference, $p < 0.01$). First the child is massaged with coconut oil and then a paste of sunnipindi and turmeric powder is used to remove the oil. Unlike many families in the traditional group, a vast majority of the families in the transitional group use bath soap, - frequently the 'Life buoy' soap - for washing the body of their children. 'Life bucy' soap is preferred because it is cheap.

Muthayya, B.C.(1972) finds that practice of using detergent soap for head bath is quite common in low class families.

Table 4.27 : Frequency of Head-bath Given to the Children According to the Income of the Family and Literacy of Mothers

Sl. No.	Income and Literacy Levels of Sugali mothers	Frequency of head-bath given to Sugali Children									
		Once in 2 days		Once in 4 dyas		Once in a week		Once in 15 days		Once in a month	
		No.	%	No.	%	No.	%	No.	%	No.	%
1. Traditional											
	Group I	4	21.0	1	52.6	3	15.7	9	47.3	2	10.5
	Group II	4	12.9	2	6.4	8	25.8	10	32.2	7	22.5
	Illiterate Mothers	7	15.6	3	6.7	10	22.2	16	35.6	9	20.0
	Literate Mothers	1	20.0	--	--	1	20.0	3	60.0	--	--
	0–1 year age child	8	53.3	3	20.0	4	26.7	--	--	--	--
	1–3 years age child	--	--	--	--	7	41.1	10	58.8	--	--
	3–5 years age child	--	--	--	--	--	--	9	50.0	9	50.0
2. Transitional											
	Group I	15	45.4	4	12.1	13	39.3	1	3.0	--	--
	Group II	3	17.6	3	17.6	6	35.2	5	29.4	--	--
	Illiterate Mothers	3	17.6	2	11.7	8	47.0	4	23.5	--	--
	Literate Mothers	15	45.4	5	15.1	11	33.3	2	6.0	--	--
	0–1 year age child	18	81.8	4	18.1	--	--	--	--	--	--
	1–3 years age child	--	--	3	18.7	11	68.7	2	12.5	--	--
	3–5 years age child	--	--	--	--	8	66.7	4	33.3	--	--

In the traditional Sugali group, it is noticed that a majority of income Group I families use hot water and bath soap for the children's bath. The majority of literate mothers in the group were found to follow a similar practice. Detergent soaps are used by income Group II families and illiterate mothers for body and head bath. A majority of mothers in income group I families and those who are literates are found to use soap nuts, turmeric powder, oil and sunnipindi during head bath.

In transitional Sugali group, irrespective of income and education all the mothers use hot water for their children's bath -Majority of income Group I families and illiterate mothers use soap nuts for head bath. Many income Group I families and literate mothers use toilet soap. A majority of Group II families and illiterate mothers use detergent soap for body and head bath. Many Group I families and literate mothers are found to use turmeric powder, oil and sunnipindi during head bath.

In traditional and transitional Sugali groups, using of toilet soap, turmeric powder, oil, sunnipindi, detergent soap and hot water are found mostly confined to the 0-1 year age group children. The use of turmeric powder, oil, sunnipindi and toilet soaps is found to decrease with advancing age of children in both the groups.

Usually the mother, grand-mother and older children give bath to their children when ever they are free mothers give bath to 58 percent of the children in the traditional group and 72 percent of the children in the transitional group. Fourteen percent of the grand mothers in traditional group and 18 percent of the grand mothers in transitional group give bath to the children. Twenty eight percent of the older children in traditional group and 10 percent of the older children in transitional group give bath to the children.

Number of Clothes to the Child

The present study reveals that 36 percent of the Sugali children in the traditional group and 16 percent of the Sugali children in the transitional group have only one pair of clothes to wear (Significant difference $p < 0.05$). Fifty six percent of the children in the traditional group and 24 percent of the children in transitional group have 2 pairs of clothes to wear (highly significant difference, $p < 0.01$), 8 percent of the children in traditional group and 48 percent of the children in transitional group have 3 pairs of clothes to wear (significant difference p<0.05) and only 12 percent of the Sugali children in the transitional group have 4 pairs.

Table 4.28 : Number of Clothes of the Children

Pairs of clothes to wear	Sugali Children		t-Value
	Tradi-tional	Transi-tional	
One Pair	36	16	2.38*
	(18)	(8)	
Two pairs	56	24	3.47**
	(28)	(12)	
Three pairs	8	48	2.28*
	(4)	(24)	
Four pairs	--	12	--
		(6)	

* p < 0.05;   ** p < 0.01

From the above data, it is seen that more than half of the children in traditional group have two pairs of clothes to wear. None of them have four pairs in this group. Where as in transitional group, nearly half of the children have three pairs and some of them have four pairs of clothes to wear. This difference with regard to number of children's clothes between traditional and transitional group may be due to income.

Table 4.29 shows that there is association between income level and number of clothes given to the child in the traditional group as well as in the transitional group. In the transitional group education of the mother also related to the number of clothes given to the child.

Frequency of Changing Children's Clothes: Poor families attach minimal importance to children's clothing, due to their low income and lack of knowledge about health and hygiene. The present study shows that 14 percent of the Sugali families in the traditional group and 38 percent of the families in the transitional group change their children's clothes once in two days (significantly different, p < 0.01), 20 percent of the families in the traditional group and 42 percent of the families in the transitional group change their children's clothes once in four days (significantly different, p < 0.05), 30 percent of the families in the traditional group and 12 percent of families in the transitional group change their children's clothes once in a week

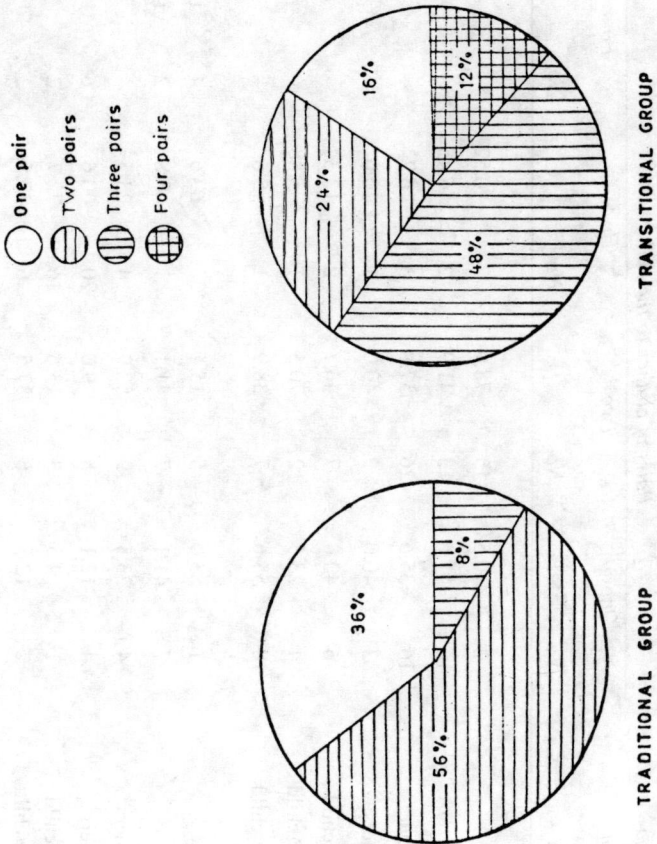

Fig. 6 : Number of Clothes to the Children

Table 4.29 : Number of Clothes to the Children According to the Income of the Family, Education of the Mother and Age of the Child

Sl. No.	Income, education Level of mothers and age of the child	Pairs of clothes to the children								X^2 value
		One		Two		Three		Four		
		No.	%	No.	%	No.	%	No.	%	
1.	**Traditional**									
	Group I	2	10.5	15	78.9	2	10.52	--	--	6.67*
	Group II	16	51.6	13	41.9	2	6.45	--	--	
	Illiterate Mothers	16	35.6	26	57.8	3	6.7	--	--	0.31
	Literate Mothers	2	40.0	2	40.0	1	20.0	--	--	
	0–1 year age child	6	40.0	7	46.7	2	13.3	--	--	2.78
	1–3 years age child	4	23.5	12	70.5	1	5.88	--	--	
	3–5 years age child	10	55.6	7	38.9	1	5.6	--	--	
2.	**Transitional**									
	Group I	1	3.0	5	15.1	23	69.6	4	12.1	16.77**
	Group II	7	41.1	7	41.1	1	5.8	2	11.7	
	Illiterate Mothers	4	23.5	9	52.9	4	23.5	--	--	12.4**
	Literate Mothers	4	12.1	3	9.0	20	60.6	6	18.1	
	0–1 year age child	1	4.5	3	13.6	16	72.7	2	9.09	8.5
	1–3 years age child	2	12.5	6	37.5	6	37.5	2	12.5	
	3–5 years age child	5	50.0	3	25.0	2	16.7	2	9.7	

* P < 0.05   ** P < 0.01

significantly different pattern in infant development prevailed while no significant difference emerged between the families in the additional income group under the different income. The present study is highly significant in this respect (p<0.01).

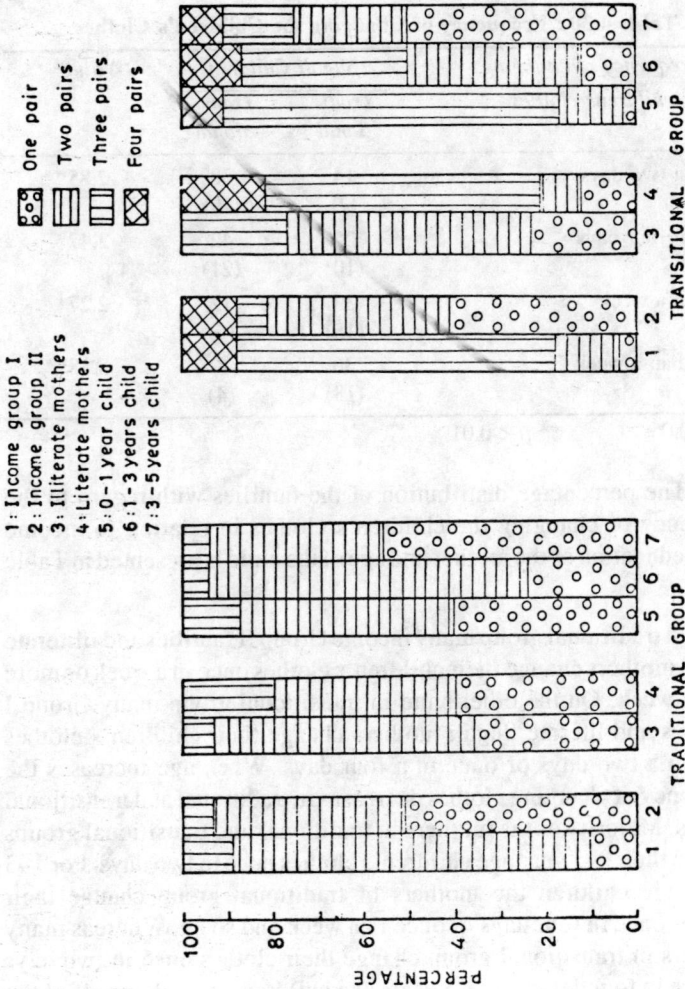

Fig. 7 : Number of Clothes to the Children according to the Income, Education of the Mother and Age of the Child

(significantly different at 0.05 percent level), 36 percent of the families in the traditional group and 8 percent of the families in the transitional group change their children's clothes after a week (highly significant difference, $p<0.01$).

Table 4.30 : Frequency of Changing the Children's Clothes

Frequency of changing childrens clothes	Sugali Children		t-Value
	Tradi-tional	Transi-tional	
Once in two days	14	38	2.85**
	(7)	(19)	
Once in four days	20	42	2.47*
	(10)	(21)	
Once in a week	30	12	2.27*
	(15)	(6)	
More than a week	36	8	3.18**
	(18)	(4)	

* $p < 0.05$;   ** $p < 0.01$

The percentage distribution of the families with regard to the frequency of changing the children's clothes in relation to income level, education of the mother and age of the child is presented in Table 4.31.

In traditional group many income Group II families and illiterate Sugali mothers change their children's clothes once in a week or more than a week. On the other hand in transitional group many Group I families and literate Sugali mothers change their children's clothes once in a two days or once in a four days. When age increases the frequency of changing clothes decreases in traditional and transitional groups. Majority of the mothers in traditional and transitional groups change their 0–1 year age children's clothes once in two days. For 1–3 years age children the mothers of traditional group change their clothes once in four days or once in a week and so on. Whereas many mothers in transitional group change their clothes once in two days or once in four days. For 3-5 years age children, more than half of the Sugali mothers in traditional group change their clothes more than a week. In transitional group more than half of the mothers are found to change their children's clothes once in four days.

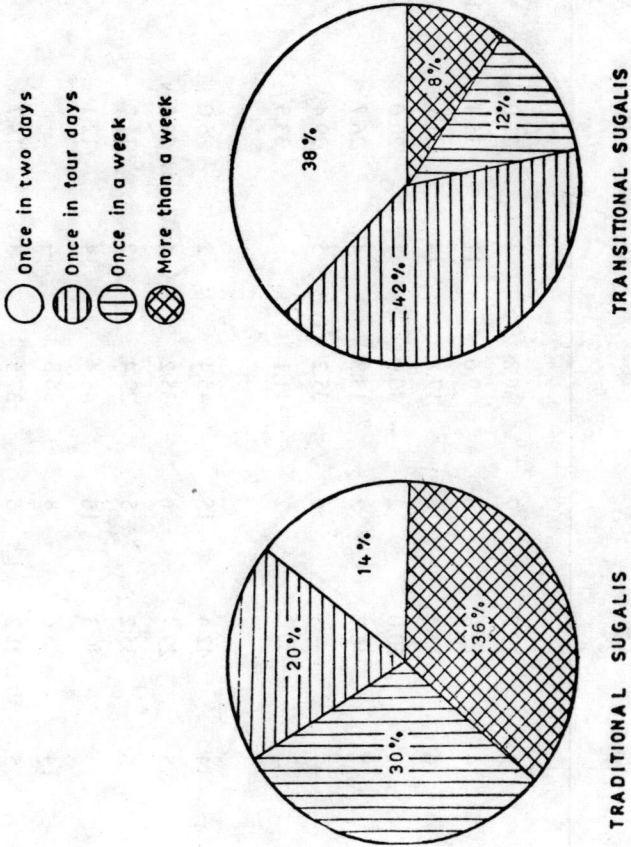

Fig. 8 : Frequency of Changing the Children's Clothes

Table 4.31 : Frequency of Changing Clothes in Relation to Income Level, Education of the Mother and Age of the Child

Sl. No.	Income, education of the mother and age of the child	Frequency of changing the Sugali childrens clothes						
		Once in two Days No. %		Once in 4 days No. %		Once in a week No. %		More than a week No. %	
		No.	%	No.	%	No.	%	No.	%
1. Traditional									
	Group I	3	15.7	7	36.8	4	21.0	5	26.3
	Group II	4	12.9	3	9.6	11	35.4	13	41.9
	Illiterate Mothers	6	13.3	8	17.8	14	31.1	17	37.8
	Literate Mothers	1	20.0	2	40.0	1	20.0	1	20.0
	0–1 year age child	7	46.7	2	13.3	4	26.7	2	13.3
	1–3 years age child	--	--	6	35.2	5	29.4	6	35.2
	3–5 years age child	--	--	2	11.1	6	33.3	10	55.6
2. Transitional									
	Group I	14	42.4	15	45.4	2	6.0	2	6.0
	Group II	5	29.4	6	35.2	4	23.5	2	11.7
	Illiterate Mothers	6	35.2	5	29.4	2	11.7	4	23.5
	Literate Mothers	13	39.3	16	48.4	4	12.1	--	--
	0–1 year age child	14	63.6	8	36.3	--	..	--	--
	1–3 years age child	5	31.2	6	37.5	3	18.7	2	12.5
	3–5 years age child	--	--	7	58.3	2	16.7	3	25.0

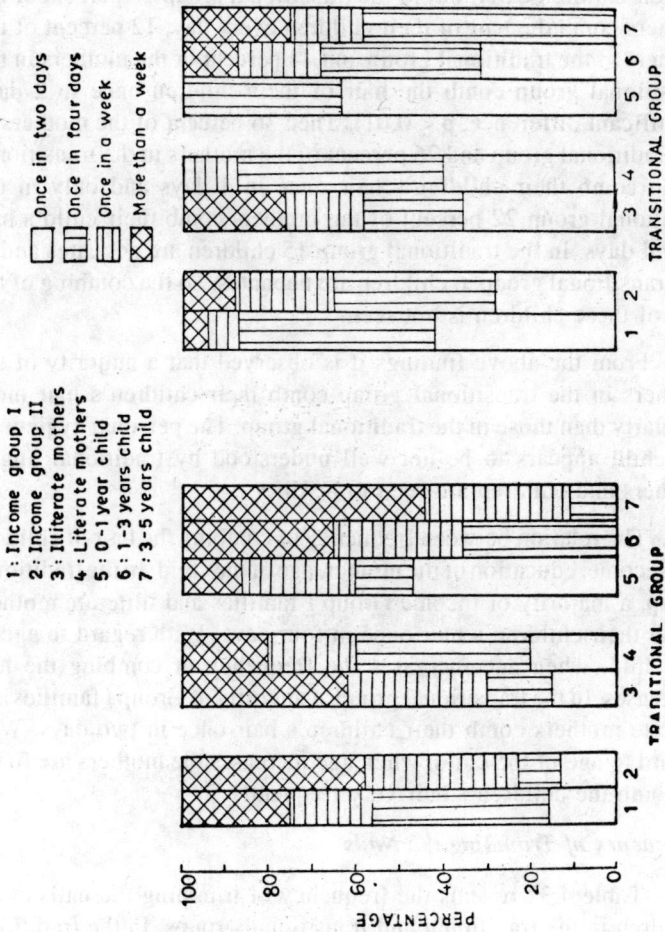

Fig. 9 : Frequency of Changing Clothes in Relation to Income, Education of the Mother and Age of the Child

Frequency of Combing the Hair

The frequency of combing the hair of the children varies from group to group. In the traditional group mothers don't comb the hair of their children daily, but in the transitional group 18 percent of the mothers comb the hair of their children every day, 12 percent of the mothers in the traditional group and 44 percent of the mothers in the transitional group comb the hair of their children once in 2 days (significant difference, $p < 0.01$). Then 36 percent of the mothers in the traditional group and 26 percent of the mothers in the transitional group comb their children's hair once in 4 days and only in the traditional group 22 percent of the mothers comb their child's hair after 4 days. In the traditional group 15 children are neonates and in the transitional group, 6 children are neonates. So the combing of the hair of these children is not seen.

From the above findings it is observed that a majority of the mothers in the transitional group comb their children's hair more regularly than those in the traditional group. The personal hygiene of the child appears to be not well understood by traditional Sugali mothers and children are seen to be dirty.

The relation between frequency of combing the hair of children and income, education of the mother, age of the child. In the traditional group, a majority of income Group I families and illiterate mothers comb their children's hair once in four days. With regard to age of the child, when age increases the frequency of combing the hair decreases. In the transitional group, a majority of Group I families and literate mothers comb their children's hair once in two days. With regard to age of the child, when age increases the mothers are found to comb the children's hair very frequently.

Frequency of Trimming the Nails

Table 4.32 reveals the frequency of trimming the nails of the children in the traditional and transitional groups. In the traditional group, 10 percent of the mothers trim the nails of children once in 15 days, 44 percent of them once in a month and 46 percent of the mothers once in two months. One the other hand, in the transitional group, 22 percent of the mothers trim the nails of their children once in 15 days, 56 percent of the mothers once in a month, 22 percent of them once in two months. There is significant difference between traditional and transitional group with respect to the frequency of trimming the nails once in two months (p < 0.01)

Table 4.32 : Frequency of Trimming the Nails of Children

Frequency of trimming the nails	Sugali Children		t-Value
	Traditional	Transitional	
Once in 15 days	10	22	1.7
	(5)	(11)	
Once in a month	44	56	1.22
	(22)	(28)	
Once in two months	46	22	2.63**
	(23)	(11)	

** p < 0.01

From the above findings, it is noticed that more them half of the transitional Sugali mothers are found to trim the nails of their children. Whereas in traditional group, nearly half of the mothers trim the nails of their children once in two months.

None of the children in either the traditional and transitional Sugali groups are trained to wash their hands before taking food.

Attitudes Towards Toilet Training to their Children

Freud emphasized the crucial importance of toilet training to the development of child's personality. The attitude of parents towards the toilet training varies from culture to culture. In some cultures it is taken casually while in some others mothers start training their children at a very young age so that cleanliness can be achieved as early as possible. However, toilet training should take into consideration physiological maturity of the child to control his bladder and bowel muscles- training if started prematurely may result in negativism, aggressiveness or timidity. On the contrary if no training is given and too casual an attitude is taken about toilet training, the child fails to understand the hygienic principles of defecation and urination.

In the present study shows that 16 percent of the respondents in the traditional group reported that there is necessity of toilet training to their children after 5 years. But in the transitional group 74 percent of the respondents were interested to give toilet training to their children after 3 years. This percentage distribution clearly shows the significant difference (p<0.01) between these two groups with regard to positive attitudes towards giving toilet training to their children. Then 84 percent of the mothers in the traditional and 26 percent of the mothers in the transitional group reported that there is no need to give toilet training to their children. There is high difference (p<0.01) between two groups.

Table 4.33 : Attitudes Towards Toilet Training to Their Children

Attitudes towards toilet training	Sugali Children		t-Value
	Tradi-tional	Transi-tional	
Necessary	16	74	7.25**
	(8)	(37)	
Not necessary	84	26	7.25**
	(42)	(13)	

** p < 0.01

On the whole, it is noticed that majority of the mothers in traditional group have not given importance to toilet training to their children when compared to the mothers in the transitional group and very few of them (16%) have shown importance to toilet training of their children and reported that it should be started after the age of 5 years.

In India, majority of the parents do not think that toilet training at an early age is important and so they tend to neglect it. Kaur, M. Sisodia, S. and Mehra, S. (1981) found that parental attitudes towards toilet training to be very casual especially in the lower classes.

In the transitional group, majority of the parents give importance to toilet training to children after 3 years. They are comparatively more educated and are very particular that their children should acquire bladder and bowl control at an early age.

Thus it is noticed that the aspect of toilet training to be offered to child or giving instructions to the child with regard to toilet training is missing in the traditional group. There is no particular age at which the child is given toilet training. Instructions regarding place for elimination are given only after the child starts walking and talking. Parents take their child's urination in the house is as natural. The child is dependent on mother to clean himself at least till 5 years of age.

In the study of Dave, P. Hakim, M. and Tavkar, N. (1984) on tribals of Gujarat revealed that there was no particular age at which the mothers toilet train the child.

In the transitional group the aspect of toilet training to the children exists to some extent. Mothers are particular to give toilet training to the child after 3 years. Instructions regarding place for elimination are given during early age itself and after defecation and place is cleaned immediately. Mother or grand mother takes care to clean the child until 5 years of age.

Table 4.34 reveals that the association between income of the family and attitudes towards toilet training to their children is absent significantly in the traditional and transitional groups. However, there is significant association ($p < 0.05$) between education of the mother and attitudes towards toilet training to the children in transitional group but not seen in the traditional group. The higher the literate mothers higher the positive attitudes towards toilet training to their children.

Table 4.34 : Attitudes of Mothers Towards Toilet Training to Their Thildren in Relation to Income of the Family and Education of the Mother

Sl. No.	Income, education of the mother	Attitude of Sugali mothers				t– Value
		Necessary		Not necessary		
		No.	%	No.	%	
1.	**Traditional**					
	Group I	3	15.7	16	84.2	
	Group II	5	16.1	26	83.8	0.132
	Illiterate Mothers	7	15.6	38	84.4	
	Literate Mothers	1	20.0	4	80.0	0.148
2.	**Transitional**					
	Group I	26	78.7	7	21.2	
	Group II	11	64.7	6	35.2	1.131
	Illiterate Mothers	7	41.17	10	58.8	
	Literate mothers	30	90.0	3	9.1	11.93**

** $P < 0.01$

Disciplinary Measures

Discipline, broadly speaking, is any kind of influence designed to help the child to learn to deal with demands from his environment that go counter to demands he might wish to make upon his environment.

Behaviours which Annoyed the Mothers

Table 4.35 shows that the traditional and the transitional mothers were annoyed with their children when they exhibited aggressive behaviour (44%, 28%), made too much noise (24%, 12%), fought with others (16%, 8%) were fussy in taking food (28%, 18%), told lies (4%, 24%), showed no progress in studies (0,44%), were dirty (0, 26%) and showed disrespect towards elders (4%, 20%). The traditional mothers were more concerned with the fights of their children. The difference between traditional and transitional mothers is significantly different.

Table 4.35 : Behaviours Which Annoyed the Mothers

Particulars	Sugali Mothers		t-Value
	Traditional	Transitional	
Aggressive behaviour	44 (22)	28 (14)	1.70
Noisy	24 (12)	12 (6)	1.6
Fights with others	16 (8)	8 (4)	4.88**
Fuss in taking food	28 (14)	18 (9)	1.20
Telling lies	4 (2)	24 (12)	1.52
Poor in studies	--	44 (22)	--
Uncleanliness	--	26 (13)	1.52
Not showing respect towards elders	4 (2)	20 (10)	1.62

** $p < 0.01$

From the above data, it is observed that a majority of traditional Sugali mothers got annoyed when their children exhibited aggressive behaviour, made too much noise, fought with others and were fussy in taking food when compared to mothers in transitional group. Very few of the traditional mothers were annoyed when their children told lies, showed no progress in studies, were dirty and showed disrespect towards elders compared to transitional mothers. This shows the mothers in traditional group give less importance to their children's education and cleanliness.

Table 4.36 reveals the percentage distribution of the Sugali mothers who were annoyed by their child's behaviour with respect to their income and their educational level. In the traditional group when income and their educational level. In the traditional group when income increases, the proportion of mothers who were annoyed by their child's behaviour also increases. In the transitional group the increase in income had just the opposite effect. Many illiterate mothers in the transitional group are seen to be annoyed by their child's behaviour like aggressive and noisy behaviour, fighting with each other and fussing about food. On the other hand many literate mothers in this group are found to be annoyed by their child's behaviour like telling lies, poor in studies, uncleanliness and disrespect towards elders.

Disciplinary Methods

Table 4.37 shows that a majority of the parents (52%) in the traditional group and 40 percent of the parents in the transitional group used scolding as a disciplinary method, 44 percent of the parents in the traditional group and 26 percent of the parents in the transitional group used spanking as a disciplinary method. More number of parents in the traditional group than those from the transitional group used scolding, spanking, deprivation of food, and physical punishment. With regard to deprivation of food and physical punishment, there is statistically significant difference between two groups. Only in the traditional group, 8 percent of the parents refrained from talking to children for disciplining their children. Only in transitional group, 8 percent of the parents were found to give advice as a method of discipline.

A majority of the parents in the traditional group used deprivation of food to the children as a disciplinary method. Apart from this

Table 4.36 : Behaviours which Annoyed the Mothers with Respect to Income and Education of the Mothers

Particulars	Sugali Mothers							
	Traditional				Transitional			
	Group I	Group II	Illiterates	Literates	Group I	Group II	Illiterates	Literates
Aggressive behaviour	57.8 (11)	35.4 (11)	46.7 (21)	20 (1)	27.2 (9)	29.4 (5)	58.8 (10)	12.1 (4)
Noisy	31.5 (6)	19.3 (6)	26.7 (12)	—	6.0 (2)	23.5 (4)	23.5 (4)	6.0 (2)
Fights with others	21.0 (4)	12.9 (4)	13.3 (6)	40 (2)	—	23.5 (4)	17.6 (3)	3.0 (1)
Fuss in taking food	31.5 (6)	25.8 (8)	28.9 (13)	20 (1)	15.1 (5)	23.5 (4)	17.6 (3)	18.1 (6)
Telling lies	—	6.4 (2)	4.4 (2)	—	24.2 (8)	23.5 (4)	11.7 (2)	30.3 (10)
Poor in studies	—	—	—	—	39.3 (13)	52.9 (9)	—	66.7 (22)
Uncleanliness	—	—	—	—	24.2 (8)	29.4 (5)	11.7 (2)	33.3 (11)
Not showing respect towards elders	5.2 (1)	3.2 (1)	2.2 (1)	20 (1)	18.1 (6)	23.5 (4)	17.6 (3)	21.2 (7)

Table 4.37 : Disciplinary Methods Used by the Parents

Particulars	Sugali Parents		t-Value
	Tradi-tional	Transi-tional	
Scolding	52 (26)	40 (20)	1.22
Spanking	44 (22)	26 (13)	1.42
Deprivation of food	36 (18)	8 (4)	3.18**
Not talking to the	8 (4)	--	--
Physical punishment	42 (21)	22 (11)	2.2*
Advice	--	16 (8)	--
Ignore	--	--	--

** $p < 0.01$ * $P < 0.05$

not talking to the child was also observed in the traditional group. Ames, E. and Randeri, K. (1965) found that Indians use rejection methods for punishment to discipline the children. In the traditional group more number of parents used physical punishment to discipline the children than transitional parents. Coleman (1976) found that the use of frequent physical punishment makes the children stubborn, depressed and confused. Bakshi, S. (1976) reported that physically punishing the children lead to reservedness, emotional instability, expediency, assertiveness and apprehensiveness.

Table 4.38 clearly shows that in the traditional group, a majority of low income (Group II) families used scolding and physical punishment than high income (Group I) families and many illiterate mothers used physical punishment as a disciplinary measure. Majority of the literate mothers used scolding and spanking as punishment. More children in the age group of 1-3 years received physical punishment than those in the 0-1 year age group and 3-5 years age group. Spanking was used more to punish the children in the 3-5 years age group than those aged 0-1 year and 1-3 years. More than half of the children in the age group of 1-3 years received punishment in the form of scolding and deprivation of food.

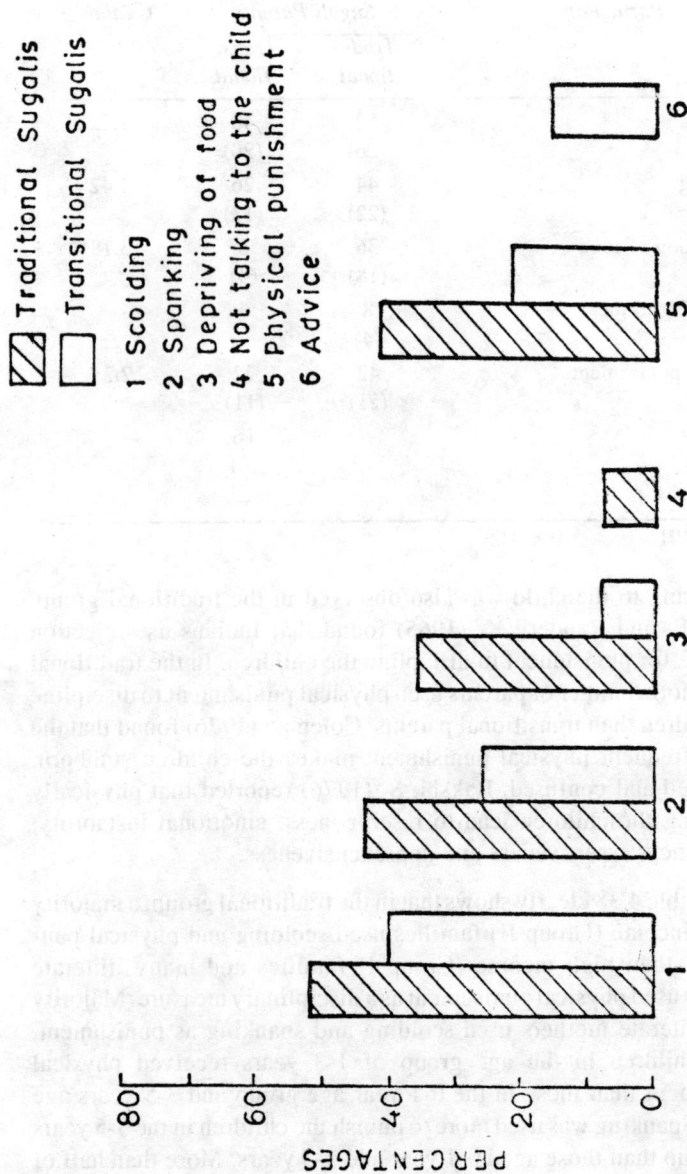

Fig. 10 : Disciplinary Methods Used by Parents

Table 4.38 : Disciplinary Methods Used by the Parents in Relation to Income of the Family, Education of the Mother and Age of the Child

Sl. No.	Particulars	Scolding	Spanking	Deprivation of food	Not talking	Physical punishment	Advice
1. Traditional
	Group I	47.3 (9)	52.6 (10)	47.3 (9)	15.7 (3)	36.8 (7)	--
	Group II	54.8 (17)	38.7 (12)	29.0 (9)	3.2 (1)	45.1 (14)	--
	Illiterate Mothers	48.9 (22)	40.0 (18)	37.8 (17)	6.7 (3)	44.4 (20)	--
	Literate Mothers	80.0 (4)	80.0 (4)	20.0 (1)	20.0 (1)	20.0 (1)	--
	0–1 year age child	60.0 (9)	26.7 (4)	--	6.7 (1)	--	--
	1–3 years age child	58.8 (10)	29.4 (5)	52.9 (9)	5.8 (1)	70.5 (12)	--
	3–5 years age child	38.9 (7)	72.2 (13)	50.0 (9)	11.1 (2)	50.0 (9)	--
2. Transitional
	Group I	39.3 (13)	18.1 (6)	--	--	6.0 (2)	21.2 (7)
	Group II	41.1 (7)	41.1 (7)	23.5 (4)	--	52.9 (9)	5.8 (1)
	Illiterate Mothers	88.2 (15)	64.7 (11)	23.5 (4)	--	64.7 (11)	11.7 (2)
	Literate Mothers	15.1 (5)	6.0 (2)	--	--	--	--
	0–1 year age child	13.6 (3)	--	--	--	--	--
	1–3 years age child	43.7 (7)	31.2 (5)	--	--	25.0 (4)	18.1 (6)
	3–5 years age child ·	83.3 (10)	66.7 (8)	33.3 (4)	--	58.3 (7)	66.7 (8)

In the transitional group, low income (Group II) families use scolding, spanking, deprivation of food and physical punishment more often than the high income (Group I) families. Majority of the illiterate mothers used scolding, spanking and physical punishment. Very few mothers in the literate group used scolding, spanking and none of them used physical punishment. Many literate mothers used advice as a technique for correcting the child's mistakes. This technique was not used in the traditional group. More children in the age group of 3-5 years received punishment like scolding, spanking, physical punishment and advice when compared to the children in the other age-groups.

On the whole physical punishment is used mostly in low income (Group II) families of the traditional and the transitional group. Rosen (1964) reported that physical punishment tends to be used by lower class parents for disciplining.

Sharma, V.P. (1981) reported in his study that highly educated mothers tended to use reasoning and persuasion. More of the less educated mothers used spanking. In the present investigation, also similar trend is observed.

Both in the traditional and transitional group, it is observed that mother is the best source of affection during early infancy. After one year of age the intensity of affection of the mother gets diluted. The child is usually looked after by the sibling, grandmother or a near relative and only with reference to the utmost needs the mother comes into field.

It is also noticed that in the traditional group often the mother is the disciplining agent, but in the transitional group few fathers are also disciplining agents.

Parental Educational Aspirations for Their Children

Most parents in India today are desirous of providing a good education to their children because, education alone enables them to secure a job, through which they can climb to a high level in the social ladder. But the actual interest shown by the parents towards their children depends on factors such as their own educational and economic status, nature of families and on many other things.

Education to the Children

Table 4.39 reveals that a majority of Sugali families in the traditional group (74%) have a negative attitude towards education of their children. A higher proportion of the families in the transitional group (86%) expressed that their children need education (It shows significant difference p<0.01).

Table 4.39 : Need for Education to the Children

Particulars	Sugali Families		t-Value
	Traditional	Transitional	
Necessary	26	86	7.69**
	(13)	(43)	
Ignore	74	14	7.69**
	(37)	(7)	

** p < 0.01

From the above findings it is observed that many Sugalis in the traditional group do not feel the necessity of educating the children. Mandal's, P.K. (1977) study on the Santhal tribe also reported similar finding. In the transitional group, many parents appears to be aware of importance of education to their children.

Table 4.40 shows that in the traditional group high income (Group I) and low income (Group II) families expressed negative

Table 4.40 : Need for Education to the Children in Relation to Income of the Family and Education of the Mother

Sl. No.	Income and education of the mother	Necessary		Not necessary		X^2-Value
		No.	%	No.	%	
1.	**Traditional**					
	Group I	7	36.84	12	63.1	
						1.86
	Group II	6	19.35	25	80.6	
	Illiterate Mothers	9	20.00	36	80.00	
						5.59*
	Literate Mothers	4	80.0	1	20.0	
2.	**Transitional**					
	Group I	28	84.8	5	15.1	
						0.01
	Group II	15	88.2	2	11.7	
	Illiterate Mothers	12	70.5	5	29.4	
						3.325
	Literate mothers	31	93.9	2	6.06	

* p < 0.05

attitude towards education of their children. In the transitional group, irrespective of their income and education of the mother, many parents stated that their children need education.

Among the parents who expressed necessity for education to their children, many of them reported that their sons should get education rather than daughters. Very few parents in the traditional (5) and in the transitional (12) stated that their daughters also need education. This shows a favourable change of attitudes towards girl's education in the transitional group.

Almost all the parents in the traditional and 72 percent of the parents in the transitional group considered education is important for getting a job and to have a steady source of income. Remaining parents in the transitional group (24%) reported that education help children to get knowledge.

From the above data it is observed that almost all the Sugalis consider education for getting a job. The 'knowledge' value of education is emphasized only by 24 percent of transitional Sugali group.

The level upto what the parents want to educate their children. Thirty percent of the parents in the traditional group, 62 percent of the parents in the transitional group reported that they would educate their children to be a literate. Sixteen percent of the traditional and 42 percent of the transitional parents indicated their desire to educate their children upto X class to take up clerical post, 10 percent of the traditional and 34 percent of the transitional parents expressed that they educate upto graduation to become elementary school teachers and none in the traditional and 20 percent in the transitional group reported that they would educate their children highly as to become professional. All these indicates significant difference between traditional and transitional groups with regard to level of educational aspirations to their children.

It is noted that none of the parent in the traditional group wanted their children to become professional. While 20 percent of the transitional parents wanted their children to become professional. When income and education of the mother increases, the level of educational aspirations also increases.

Future Ambitions about Children

Table 4.41 reveals that the future ambitions about male children in the traditional and transitional groups. More than half of the parents in the traditional (58%) and 36 percent of the parents in the transitional group reported that their sons should work hard (it shows significant difference $p<0.05$). Twenty six percent in the traditional and 72 percent in the transitional group expressed that their sons should be well educated and well employed. Twenty two percent of the traditional and 40 percent of the transitional Sugalis reported that their sons should not become drunkards. Eighty percent in the traditional and 44 percent in the transitional group wanted their children to be disassociated with the tribal culture and it's setting.

Table 4.41 : Future Ambitions about Male Children by Sugalis

Particulars	Sugali parents		t-Value
	Traditional	Transitional	
Hard worker	58	36	2.29*
	(29)	(18)	
Educated to read and write	20	10	1.42
	(10)	(5)	
Well adjusted in home	12	28	2.05*
	(6)	(14)	
Well educated	26	72	5.22**
	(13)	(36)	
Good employee	26	72	5.22**
	(13)	(36)	
Should not drink	22	40	2.0*
	(11)	(20)	
Should live out of tribal culture	8	44	2.58**
	(4)	(22)	

* $p < 0.05$;   ** $p < 0.01$

From the above data, it is interesting to note that a majority of the traditional parents are not found to give importance to education of their sons. The illiteracy of the parents may be partly responsible for this situation.

In the transitional group, a majority of parents are found to give emphasis to well education and employment to their sons. They also reported that their children should be well adjusted in home, should not drink and live out of their culture. It shows social transformation of Sugalis.

In the traditional group, when income and education of the mother increases, the ambitions of parents for their children's education and employment also increases. They also wish their children not to cultivate undesirable social habits like drinking which is highly prevalent among the Sugalis. For this reason, they prefer their children to leave all attachment to the tribal culture. In many less income (Group II) families and illiterate mothers have ambitions about their sons as hard working labourers. In the transitional group, irrespective of income and education of the mother the ambitions of parents related to education, employment, and personal habits is high.

Table 4.42 shows the future ambitions about female children in the traditional and transitional groups. Thirty six percent of the parents in the traditional group, 24 percent of the parents in the transitional group expressed that their daughters should become physically strong and work hard. Ten percent of the traditional and 40 percent of the transitional Sugalis stated that their female children should get education to read and write. (It shows significant difference $p<0.01$). Thirty two percent of the traditional and 54 percent of the transitional group parents reported that their daughters should get well adjusted in home. Twenty eight percent of the traditional and 36 percent of the transitional Sugalis expressed their ambition to become good housewives. None of them in the traditional 20 percent of them in the transitional group reported that their daughters should become good employees.

Table 4.42 : Future Ambitions about Female Children by Sugalis

Particulars	Sugali Families		t-Value
	Traditional	Transitional	
Hard worker	36	24	1.33
	(18)	(12)	
Educated to read and write	10	40	3.70**
	(5)	(20)	
Well adjusted in home	32	54	2.31*
	(16)	(27)	
Good housewife	28	36	0.86
	(14)	(18)	
Good employee	--	20	--
		(10)	

** p < 0.01   *p < 0.05

From the above findings, it is noted that very few parents in the traditional group expressed that their daughters should educate to read and write. The corresponding proportion in the transitional group is high. None of the parent in the traditional group have ambition to educate the female children to take up a job. But some in the transitional group want their daughters to take up jobs. Hence there is a need to organise educational programmes to motivate the groups to learn and to realize the importance of education.

The future ambitions about female children in relation to income and education of the mother. In the traditional group, many income Group I families and literate mothers are found to have ambitions to educate their daughters, to train them to get well adjusted in home and to become good housewife. A majority of those in income Group II families and illiterate mothers are found to have the ambition to see their daughters as hard working labourers.

In the transitional group irrespective of income and education, the mothers have ambitions as to get their daughters literates and to help them to get well adjusted in home to become good housewives and even take up a good job, but majority of those in income Group II families where mothers are illiterate, the ambition for female children is to make them to become hard working labourers.

A majority of parents (72%) in the traditional group expressed that they do not have a desire to live with children during old age. The corresponding proportion in the transitional group is 60 percent. The remaining parents who have a desire to live with children during old age, also expressed that they want to stay with their sons only.

It is observed that in the Sugali community the custom of living with children during old age is not prevalent. That is why a majority of the parents are not willing to live with children.

Greater proportion of traditional Sugalis expressed that the Government has to support and take the responsibility of their children's future. Majority of them indicated that the Government should provide all the facilities to promote male children's education and employment rather than female children's education and employment. In the transitional group, a majority of parents expressed that they (parents) should take the responsibility regarding the children's future but that the Government should provide help for the same. In the traditional group, due to their illiteracy and lack of exposure to urbanization, lack of knowledge, majority of them are not aware of the tribal welfare programmes undertaken by the Government and voluntary organisations.

As a result they are not utilizing the available services properly.

The transitional group on the other hand, due to better education, greater contact with other communities and urban centres they are aware of the programmes implemented by the Government and majority of them are utilizing the services properly.

5
Summary and Conclusions

The main objective of the present study was to study child rearing practices among traditional and transitional Sugali community from birth to 5 years of age. The area selected for the study was 'Sugalimitta', Chittoor District, Andhra Pradesh. A sample of 50 traditional Sugali families from Peddathanda, Nallaguttapalli thanda and 50 transitional Sugali families from Chinnathanda were selected. All the selected families had atleast one child in the age group 0-5 years.

Several aspects of child care were taken into consideration while preparing the schedule. Information was collected from mothers about the general background, marriage and family and child rearing practices specifically, religious ceremonies performed on children, feeding practices, health and hygienic practices, Disciplinary measures and parental educational aspirations for their children. The necessary information was collected by using an interview schedule and through observation. The data thus collected was pooled and percentages for various items of information were calculated. The significant difference between traditional and transitional Sugali groups in the observed findings was estimated through the age of t-test for proportions. To find out the effect of income, education of the mother and age of the child on the child rearing practices of the groups on the observed data, the chi-square was used.

The main inference drawn from the present study are as follows:

1. A majority of the families in the traditional and transitional groups are of the nuclear type.

2. A vast majority of the traditional Sugalis are engaged in their traditional occupations but many of the Sugalis in transition are primarily dependent on salaried jobs with regular income.

3. The annual income of a majority of the traditional Sugalis is below Rs. 2000/- while that a majority of the transitional Sugalis is more than Rs. 2000/-

4. Many of the parents in the traditional Sugali group are illiterates

5. Traditional Sugali families keeps the surroundings dirty compared to transitional Sugali families.

6. A majority of the traditional Sugali women were found to marry at the age of 16-18 years, but in the transitional group the age at marriage of Sugali women was increased.

7. Matrilateral cross-cousin marriages are mostly seen in the Sugalis, but a decreasing trend in the proportion of consanguineous marriages is observed from traditional to transitional Sugalis.

8. The traditional and transitional Sugalis, practice pregnancy taboos relating to food and movement.

9. There is less birth spacing in the traditional Sugali women as compared to transitional Sugali women.

10. Higher number of spontaneous abortions were found to occur in the traditional Sugali women than transitional Sugali women.

11. A majority of the women in the traditional group desire to have large family size (4 or 5 children) whereas in the transitional group, greater proportion of women are desirous of having small size (2 or 3 children) families.

12. The preference for son as first child is very much intact in the both groups.

13. To limit family size a majority of transitional Sugali women proposed to undergo birth control measures mainly tubectomy operations when compared to traditional Sugali women.

14. In the traditional group, two ceremonies are performed when women conceive for the first time but in the transitional group it is not customarily practiced. A majority of traditional families perform purificatory ceremony after child's birth. Ceremony associated with birth of a male child, cradling, name giving, tonsure ceremony for their children are performed by both the groups. In the traditional group, income of the family is associated with performance of ceremonies. In the transitional group, education of the mother is associated.

15. Breast feeding is found to be universal and a majority of women in both the groups initiated on the first day after birth.

16. Honey is the first oral feed which is used in a majority of the traditional and transitional families.

17. Irrespective of income and education of the mother, a majority of the traditional Sugali women practice prolonged breast feeding. In the transitional group, when income and education of the mother increases, the duration of breast feeding is less.

18. A majority of children received cow's and goat's milk as substitutes for breast milk and only few in the transitional group received the commercial preparations.

19. More number of traditional Sugali mothers started supplementary feeding for their children between 1 and 1½ year. Many mothers in the transitional group started giving supplementary foods at 7-12 months of age with increase in income and education, the mothers are found to seen with introducing the supplementary foods at an early age (Before 6 moths, 7-12 months).

20. A greater proportion of children in the traditional group are found to suffer from cold, cough, diarrhoeas, scabies, measles when compared to children in the transitional group.

21. The indigenous and magical treatment is very much prevalent in the traditional group than transitional group. There is increase in trend with regard to allopathic treatment from traditional to transitional group.

22. In the traditional Sugali families, the immunization status of the children is unsatisfactory compared to the children in the

transitional Sugali families.

23. In the traditional group, a majority of the children have not regularly cleaned their teeth compared to the transitional group. When educational level of the mother increases, the cleaning of teeth by children also increases.

24. In both the groups, as the education of mother and income decreases the children were found to have bath less frequently and vice-versa. When age of the child increases they were found to have bath less frequently.

25. More than half of the children in the traditional group have two pairs of clothes to wear. None of them have four pairs, whereas in transitional groups, nearly half of the children have three pairs and some have four pairs of clothes. There is association between income, education of the mother and number of clothes given to the child. When income, education of the mother increases, the frequency of changing clothes increases. When age increases, the frequency of changing clothes decreases in the traditional and transitional groups.

26. A majority of the mothers in traditional group have not given importance to toilet training to their children. In the transitional group, the higher the literate mothers, higher the positive attitudes towards toilet training their children.

27. A larger proportion of parents in the traditional group, than those from the transitional group use scolding, spanking, deprivation of food and physical punishment. In both the groups, low income and illiterate mothers use scolding, spanking, deprivation of food and physical punishment more often than the high income and literate mothers. Many literates in the transitional group use advice as a technique for discipline.

28. In the traditional group, many parents are not found to give importance to education of their sons and daughters. In the transitional group, a majority of parents are found to give emphasis to well education and employment to their sons and daughters. They also wish their children not to cultivate undesirable social habits.

Recommendations for Further Research

1. A case study method can be adopted to study and to have a clear picture of the child rearing practices in traditional and transitional Sugali groups.

2. A long-term study on the child rearing practices and their influence on the personality development can be conducted.

3. A comparative study can be undertaken to find out the differences or similarities in the child rearing practices of the transitional Sugalis and the Hindu communities of Chittoor district, Andhra Pradesh.

Bibliography

Agarwal, D.K., Agarwal, K.N. and Khare, B.B. (1985) 'Study on current status of infant and childhood feeding practices', *Indian Pediatrics*, Vol. 20, p. 716.

Ahuja, R. (1966) 'Marriage among the Bhils' *Man in India*, Vol. 46 No. 3, pp. 233-239.

Ames, E. and Randeri, K.(1965) 'Some differences in the childrearing practices of Indian and Canadian Mothers', *Indian Psychological Review*, Vol. 2, No.1, pp. 15-18.

A.P.A.U. Report (1983) 'Profile of Tribal families in East Godavari District' Integrated Tribal Development Agency, Hyderabad, pp. 38-54.

Aphale, C. (1976) '*Growing up in an urban complex*' National Publishing House, New Delhi, pp. 135-167.

Ayer, M.E. and Bernreuter, R.A. (1951) 'A study of the relationship between discipline and personality traits in young children.' *Journal of Genetic Psychology*, Vol. 50, pp. 165-170.

Bahadur, K.P. (1977) '*Caste, tribes and culture of India, Andhra Pradesh, Madhya Pradesh and Maharashtra*', Vol. II, Ess Ess Publications, Delhi, pp. 61-74.

Behl, L. (1979) 'Some aspects of Infant rearing practices and beliefs of tribal inhabitants of Himachal Pradesh' *Indian Pediatrics*,

Vol. 16, No. 4, pp. 337-341.

Bailure, A. (1971) '*Food consumption patterns of preschool children in India*' I Asian Congress of Nutrition, Hyderabad, p. 256.

Basu, M.P. (1970) 'Some aspects of the Banjara' *Tribe*, Vol, VI, No. 4, pp. 16-17.

Basu, S.K. (1977) 'Consanguinity study among the Muslim Dawoodi Bhords of Udaipur' Rajasthan Proc. of 4th Annual Conference of Indian Society of Human Genetics, Madras.

Belavady B. et al (1959) 'Studies on lactationand dietary habits of the Nilgiri Hill Tribes' *Indian Journal of Medical Research*, Vol. 47, No.2, pp. 221-233.

Bhandari, N.R. and Patel, G.P. (1973) 'Dietary and feeding habits of infants in various socio-economic groups'. *Indian Pediatrics*, Vol.10, No.4, pp. 233-238.

Bhogle, S. (1978) 'Child rearing practices among three cultures' *Social Change*, Vol. 8, No.3, pp. 6-12.

Cameron, M. and Hofvander, Y. (1983) '*Manual on feeding infants and young children*', Oxford Medical Publications (FAO/WHO/UNICEF).

Census of India (1961) Monograph Series Part V-B (IV), Lambadi (A Scheduled Tribe of Andhra Pradesh) *Ethnographic Study*, No. 17, New Delhi.

Census of India (1971) Series 2 Andhra Pradesh Part II-C (i) Social and cultural tables and Part V-A Special tables on Scheduled castes and Scheduled tribes, Controller of Publictions, Delhi.

Chowdhuri, M.K., De, S. and Debnath, A. (1985) 'Impact of prevalent diseases among the tribals of tribal concentrated areas of West Bengal.' Chaudhuri, B. (ed) *Tribal health: Socio-cultural dimensions* Inter India Publications, pp. 124-133.

Coleman, C.J. (1976) '*Abnormal psychology and Human life*'. Taroporvala Sons & Co., Private Ltd., Bombay, pp. 548-550.

Dabi, D.R., Singh, R.N. and Gupta, D.D. (1983) 'Family size and immunization status of the underfive children' *Indian Journal of Pediatrics*, Vol. 50, No. 406, pp. 503-504.

Das, K. and Ghosh, A.K. (1985) 'Child Health Care: A Study on the Santhals of Bihar' Chaudhuri, B. (ed) *Tribal Health: Socio-cultural Dimensions*, Inter India Publications, New Delhi, pp. 148-152.

Das, R.K. (1972) 'Marriage and Kinship among the Kabui Nagas of Manipur', Man in India, Vol. 52, No. 3, pp. 228–229.

Dash, J. (1985) 'The concept and treatment of disease in tribal Orissa' Chaudhuri, B. (ed.) Tribal health : Socio-cultural Dimensions Inter India Publications, New Delhi, pp. 217–221.

Datta Banik, N.D. (1975) 'Breast feeding and weaning practices of pre-school children in an urban community in Delhi', Indian Pediatrics, Vol. 12, No. 7, pp. 569–574.

Dave, C. (1985) 'Infant feeding practices in tribal pockets of Udipur' Social Welfare, Voi. XXXII, No. 3, p. 27.

Dave, C. and Sadashivaiah, K. (1981) 'Family size and quality of life' Social Change, Vol. II, pp. 35–44.

Dave, P., Hakim, M. and Tavkar, N. (1984) 'Child care amongst the tribals of Gujarat', ICCW News Bulletin, Vol. XXXII, No. 7, pp. 11–14.

Desai, A.R. (1977) 'Tribes in transition' Romesh Thapur (ed.) Tribe, caste and religion in India, The Macmillan Company of India Ltd., Meerut, pp. 16–27.

Devadas, R.P. (1968) 'Social and Cultural factors influencing malnutrition'. Proc. Nutri. Soci. India, No. 6.

Devadas, R.P. and Easwaran, P.P. (1986) 'Intra family food intake of selected rural households and food consumption pattern of pregnant women. *The Indian Journal of Nutrition and Dietetics*, Vol. 23, No. 12, pp. 345-346.

Devis cited by Calavano, N.A. (1982) 'Infant mortality and morbidity in relation to feeding practices' *Baroda Journal of Nutrition*, 9, pp. 138-143.

Dube, L., (1949) 'Pregnancy and Child birth among the Amat Gonds'. *The Eastern Anthropologist*, Vol.2, No. 3, pp. 153-159.

Dube, S.C. (1958) *'India's Changing Villages A Rural Development*

126   *Child Rearing Practices in Tribals*

Project in Action' Routledge and Kegan Paul Ltd., London, pp. 52-54.

Editorial Source (1986) 'Reduction of poverty among Scheduled tribes' *Vanyajati*, Vol. XXXIV, No. 2, pp. 1-2.

Freedman, R. and Whelpton, P.K. (1950) 'Fertility planning and Fertility rates by religious interest and denomination' *Social and psychological factors affecting fertility'*, New York Milbank Memorial Fund, Vol. 2.

Gosh, B.N. (1966) 'Feeding habits of infants and children in South India, *Indian Journal of Medical Research*, Vol. 54, No.9, pp. 889-897.

Grantham-McGregor, S. Landman, J. and Desai, P. (1982) 'Child rearing in poor urban Jamaica' *Child Care Health and Development and Multidisciplinary Journal*, Vol.9, No. 2, p.65.

Grover, S. (1977) 'Parental aspirations as related to personality and school achievements of children' Punjab University, Ph.D. Thesis (unpublished).

Gurumurthy, G. (1984) 'Culture and Fertility Among Yanadis: A Tribal Community in South India' *The Eastern Anthropologist*, Vol. 39, No. 1, pp. 35-40.

Hemalatha Rani, P. (1980) 'Health and Hygiene among Valmiki' A unpublished dissertation submitted to S.V. University for the award of the degree of Master of Arts in Social Anthropology, pp. 35-50.

Hurlock, E.B. (1978) '*Child Development'* McGrew Hill Book Company, New York, pp. 289-296.

--------(1980) '*Developmental Psychology'* McGrew Hill Book Company, New York, pp. 91-95.

Indira Bai, K., et al. (1981) ' A comparative study of feeding patterns of infants in rural and urban areas near Tirupati' *Indian Journal of Pediatrics*, Vol., 49, No. 392, pp. 277-281.

Jaiswal, Srinivas Cited by Gurumurthy, G. (1984) 'Culture and fertility among Yanadis' *The Eastern Anthropologist*, Vol. 39, No.1, pp. 35-42.

Jha, M. (1973) 'A Study of the Ollar of Orissa; Readings in Tribal Culture. Inter India Publications, New Delhi, pp. 87-89. 143-147.

Joshi, D.C. (1982) 'Educational problems of the Scheduled castes and Scheduled tribes of Baroda District'. *Indian dissertation Abstracts*, Vol. XI, No3 and 4, ICSSR, New Delhi, pp. 6-60.

Kakar, S. (1979) 'The inner world"—*Mothers and infants, International Social Science Journal*, Vol. 31, No.3, pp. 440-446.

Kaur, M., Sisodia, G.S. and Mehra, S. (1979) 'Customary practices observed in birth and upbringing of children', A Study ,of a Village in Haryana, *Indian Journal of Social Work*, Vol.42, pp. 75-110.

Kohn, M.L. and Carroll, E.E. (1966) 'Social class and the allocation of parental responsibilities' *Socimetry*, Vol.23, pp. 372-392.

Lahiri, S. (1974) 'Preference for sons and ideal family in urban India' *Journal of Indian Social Work*, Vol. 34, pp. 232-335.

Madhavi, J.(1979) 'Health and Hygiene among the Yeukulas and Chenchus of Ahobilam in Kurnool district' An unpublished dissertation submitted to S.V. University for the award of the degree of master of Arts in Social Anthropology, pp. 6-7 and 30-35.

Madhavi, V. Rao, P.N. and Mathew, Y.C. (1972) 'A Survey of Infant feeding and weaning practices in the village Fatehpur'- Hyderabad. *Indian Pediatrics*. Vol. IX, No.8, pp. 480-483.

Mahanta, K.C. (1977) 'Socio-ecnoomic aspects of the Nocte marriage system', *Vanyajati*, Vol. XXV, No.1, pp.2-7.

Mahboob Hussain, S.K. (1951) 'Koyas' *Man in India*, Vol. 31, No. 1, pp. 33-37.

Maidya, R.N. et al (1970) 'Influence of Socio-economic and environmental factors on birth weight' *Indian Journal of Medical Research*, Vol, 58, No. 5, pp. 651-660.

Majumder, B. (1986) 'Culture change among the Totos' *Man and Life*, Vol. 12, No. 1 and 2,p. 82.

Mandal, P.K. (1977) 'Traditional and Modernity among the Santhals-

A Micro Study' *Vanyajati*, Vol. XXV, No.4, pp. 25-26.

Masani cited by Mathew, A. (1982) 'How effective is the radio in educating rural mothers'? *The Indian Journal of Home Science*, Vol. 14, No.3, pp. 21-23.

Meinzen, R.S. (1980) 'Norms and realities of marriage arrangments in a South Indian Town'. *Economic and Political Weekly*, No. 27-39, p.1137.

Minturn, L. and Hitchcock, J.T. (1964) 'The Rajputs of Khalapur, India'. Whiting, B.B. (ed) *'Six cultures: Studies of Child rearing'* John Wiley and Sons, Inc., pp. 280-311.

Mudgal, S., Rajput, V.S., et al (1979) 'Tribals of Madhya Pradesh, Knowledge, attitude and practice, Survey of Infant Feeding Practices'. *Indian Pediatrics*, Vol. 16 pp. 617-620.

Mukhopadhyay, R. (1984) 'Dilemma of Tribal Transformation: The case of Chenchus'. *Vanyajati*, Vol. XXXII, No. 2, pp. 21-22.

Mundri, L.S. (1965) 'A Munde Birth' *Man in India*, Vol. 36, No.2, pp. 56-71.

Muthayya, B.C. (1972) 'Child Welfare' Existing Conditions and Parental Attitudes, A Purposive Study in Andhra Pradesh. National Institute of Community Development, pp. 60-77.

Nag, M.K. (1954) 'A demographic study of the Kanikkar of Travancore'. *Bulletin of the Department of Anthropology*, Government of India, Calcutta, Vol. II, No, 2, pp. 95-115.

Nagabhushanamama, K. (1984) 'Parent-child Interaction in the Harijan community during pre-school period i.e., two to five years' An unpublished dissertation submitted to S.V. University in partial fulfilment of the requirements of the Degree of Master of Science in Home Science, pp. 50-62 and 85-87.

Baik, S. and Sharma, A.K. (1985) 'Social structure and family planning: A case study of two tribal villages'. *The Journal of Family Welfare*, Vol.XXII, No.1, pp. 54-57.

Narahari, S. (1982) 'A gentic study among the Yerukulas of Ananra Pradesh (India)' Ph.D. thesis, S.V. University, Tirupati.

(1985) 'An Ethnogrpahic note of a Nomadic tribe: Nakkala, Southern

India, *Vanyajati*, Vol, XXX, No. 4, p. 10.

Narayan, S. (1983) 'Health Care of the Oreon Children' *Social Welfare*, Vol, XXX, No 1, pp. 17-18.

NIN Annual Report 1982 'National Institute of Nutrition, Hyderabad.

Nirmala, K. et. al (1981) 'Feeding patterns of infants in Devangers' *The Indian Journal of Pediatrics*, Vol. 49, No, 392, pp. 281-285.

Pandey, D.N., Agnihotri, S.N. and Srivastava, A.K. (1979) 'Immunization practices among children' *Indian Psychological Review*. Vol. 18, No. 1-4, pp. 112-116.

Pandu Ranga Swamy, K. (1983) 'Population structure of Sugalis of Kurnool District of Andhra Pradesh' Dissertation submitted to S.V. University, Tirupati for the award of the Degree of Master of Science in Physical Anthropology, pp. 21-22.

Park cited by Kapoor, S. and Moudgil, A.C. (1984) 'Factore influencing induced abortion in a rural setting with particular reference to indigenous methods'. *Indian Journal of Clinical Psychology*, Vol. II, No.1, p.41.

Park, S. K. and Park, K. (1980) 'Text-book of preventive and Social Medicine 8th edition Messns Banarsidas Bhanot Publishers, Jabalpur.

Patodi, R.K., et. all (1976) 'Infant feeding practics in urban and rural areas in Madhya Pradesh' *The Indian Journal of Pediatrics*, Vol, 43, No, 346, pp. 333-338.

Pratap, D.R. (1968) 'The Banjaras of Bapunagar (A settlement in the urban environs of Hyderabad), Andhra Pradesh, Tribal Research and Training Institute.

Prathyusha, K. (1985) 'A Study on child rearing practices in Harijan community (Madiga) An unpublished dissertation submitted to S. V. University in partial fulfilment of the requirements of the Degree of Master of Science in Home Science, pp. 53-58.

Puri, R.K. et. al (1976) 'Infant feeding and child rearing methods in Pondicherry, South Inida'. *The Indian Journal of Pediatrics*, Vol. 43, No. 346, pp. 323-333.

Puri, R.K., Verma, I.C., and Bhargava, I (1978) Effects of consanguin-

ity in a community in Pondicherry- *Medical Genetics in India,*
2 Ed. (Varma, I.C.) Auroma Enterprises Pondicherry.

Radke, M.J. (1946) 'The relation of parental authority to children's
behaviour and attitudes' *Minneapolis*: Univ. Minnesota Press.

Raghavaaiah, V. (1972) 'Tribes of India' *Bharatiya Adimijati Sevak
Sangh,* New Delhi, Vol.II, pp. 385-387.

Rajalakshmi, M. (1979) 'Breast feeding and weaning in two Indian
villages', *Anthropological Survey of India,* Mysore, India, pp.
38-44.

Ramachandra Reddy, M. (1984) 'Population Structure and Family
Planning in the Sugalis, A tribal Population of Andhra Pradesh'
A Dissertation submitted to partial fulfilment for the award of
Degree of M.Phil in Population Studies, S.V. University, Tirupati.

Rao, M. (1985) 'Food beliefs of rural women during reproductive
years in Dharwad, India', *Ecol. of Food and Nutri,* Vol. 16., pp.
93-103.

Reddy, A.B. (1977) 'Life cycle ceremonies among the Yerukulas of
Ahobilam, Kurnool District.' An unpublished dissertation submitted to S.V. University, in partial fulfilment of requirements
for the Degree of Master of Arts in Social Anthropology, pp. 48-
53.

Reddy, S.B. (1977) 'Life cycle ceremonies among the Muttarasi of
Chittoor district' An unpublished dissertation submitted to S.V.
University, Tirupati in partial fulfilment of requirements for the
Degree in Master of Arts in Social Anthropology, pp. 28-32.

Reddy, S.V.B. and Reddy, S.P. (1979) 'Life cycle ceremonis among
the Jalaries of Coastal Andhra' *Vanyajati,* Vol. 27 No.3, pp. 10-
12.

Reddy, P.C. (1983) 'consanguinity and imbreeding effects on fertility,
mortality and morbidity in the Malas of Chittoor district'.
Z.Morph. Anthrop. 74. pp. 45-51.

Reichel, A.D. (1979) 'Child rearing in a Colombian Village' *International Social Science Journal,* Vol. 31 No.3, pp. 420-424.

Rizvi, S.N.H. (1985) 'Health practices of the Jaunsaris - A socio-
cultural Analysis' Chaudhuri, B. *Tribal Health: Socio-cultural
Dimensions,* Inter India Publications, p. 232.

Rohini, A. and Reddy, G.G. (1985) 'Some Demographic trends among the tribal women of Andhra Pradesh', *Man and life*, Vol, II, No. 1 and 2, pp. 89-94.

Roy, S.C., Majumdar, D.N. and Elwin, V. cited by Choudhuri, B. and Chaudhuri, S. (1985) 'Tribal Health, Disease and Treatment: A Review study'. Chaudhuri, B. (ed.) *Tribal health: Socio-cultural Dimensions* Inter India Publications, New Delhi, pp. 39-40.

Roy Burman, B.K. et. al, (1961) 'Ethnographic Notes on Yerukula, Boyas, Nirshikaris and Bala Santhosha in A.P. ', Vol. II, Part V B (8), Office of the Director of Census Operations, Hyderabad & Census of Inida, NDI-16.

Roychoudary, A.K. (1976) 'Imbreeding in Indian Populations' Trans, Bose, Res. Inst. (39) pp. 65-76.

Saibaba, K. (1977) 'Life cycle ceremonis among the Boyas of Nayudupet (Nallore Dt.) Andhra Pradesh'. An unpublished dissertation submitted to S.V. University for the award of the Degree of Master of Arts in Social Anthropology, pp. 19-23.

Samanta, R.K. and Shyam Sunder, L. (1985) The lambadis: Their socio-psychological and Agro-economic characteristics. *Man in India*, Vol. 65, No.3, pp. 269-277.

Sampath, R. (1964) 'Child care and child rearing among the Gonds of Tamis'. *The Indian Journal of Social Work*, Vol. 24, No.4, pp. 281-286.

Saraswathi, S. (1978) 'Customs and beliefs associated with pregnancy and child birth in rural Orissa'. *The Indian Journal of Social Work*, Vol. 39, No.1, pp. 79-84.

Sarker, A., Choudhuri, N. and Sankar Roy, G. (1955) 'Birth and Pregnancy rites among the Oraons'. *Man in India*, Vol. 35, No.1, pp. 46-51.

Sears, R.R. Maccoby, E.E. and Levin, H.R. (1957) '*Patterns of child rearing*' New York, Peterson & Co., pp. 457-458 and 480-481.

Sharma, V.P. (1981) '*Indian Urban Families: Child rearing practices and child growth*', National Council of Educational Research and Training, New Delhi, pp. 26-30.

Shrivastav, A. (1986) 'Tribal habitats under the impact of urbanization and Industrialisation'. *Man and Life*, Vol. 12, No. 1 and 2, pp. 69-76.

Sibajuddin, S. M. (1984) 'Reproduction and consanguinity among Chenchus of Andhra Pradesh'. *Man in India*, Vol. 64, No.2, p. 188-190.

Sidana, U.R.and Sinha, D. (1973) 'Child-rearing practices and the development of fears in children' *Psychological Studies* Vol. 18, No.2, pp. 50-60.

Singh, R. (1987) 'Marriage and law among the Bhils of Rajasthan'. *The Eastern Anthropologist*, Vol. 40, No.2, p.89.

Singh, M.B. and Daur, S. (1981) 'Mother-child interaction in rural and urban areas. *Indian Psychological Review*, Vol. 20. No.2, pp. 7-16.

Sinha, R.K. (1984) 'Birth-rites and rituals among the Bhilala', *Vanyajati*, Volo. XXXII, No.3, pp.5-8.

Sinha, R.K. (1977) 'Family composition among the Pando tribe', *Vanyajati*, Vol. XXV, No.3, pp. 23-25.

Sinha. U.P. (1984) 'Sex-composition and Differential mortality among tribals of India'., *The Indian Journal of Social Work.* Vol. XLIV, No.4, P.No. 387-391.

Sobhavathi, J. (1980) 'Health and Hygiene among the Harijans of Charala'. An unpublished dissertation submitted to S.V. University for the award of the Degree of Master of Arts in Social Anthropology, pp. 29-36 and 60-65.

Suvarna Devi, P. and Behera, P.L. (1980) 'A study of breast feeding practices in South India, *Indian Pediatrics*, Vol. 17, pp. 753-756.

Swain, L. (1985) 'Santal tribes: Infant feeding practices', *Social Welfare*, Vol. XXXII, No.3, pp. 22-23.

Swaroop, R. (1963) 'All about pregnancy, child birth and baby care Madhuri Publishers, 15, Gokhale Marg, Lucknow, (India), p.28.

Thurston, E.A. (1909) 'Castes and Tribes of Southern India, Vol. IV (K to M) Government Press, Madras, pp. 219–232.

Usha Rani, K. (1980) 'Life cycle ceremonies among the Mala of Charala (Chittoor district)' An unpublished dissertation submitted to S.V. University for the award of the Degree of Master of Arts in Social Anthropology, pp. 25-51.

Venkatachalam, P.S. (1982) 'Nutrition for mother and Child', *NIN Publication Series*, pp. 21-30.

Venkatachalam, P.S. and Rebello, L.M. cited by Khan, M.E., Prasad, CVS, and Majumdar, A. (1981) *Health Practices in two States of India Social Change*, Vol. II, p.18.

Vidyarthi, L.P. Rai, B.K. (1976) '*The tribal culture of India*', Concept Publishing Company, New Delhi, pp. 279-307 and 454-472.

Vijay, H., Ghosh, S. et.al (1976) 'Immunization Status in an Urban Community', *Indian Pediatrics*, Vol. XIII, No.10, pp. 747-750.

Vimala, V. Ratnaprabha, C. Unpublished 'Infant feeding practices prevalent among tribal communities of Bhadragiri, Vizianagaram Dt. Andhra Pradesh', Project Report by A.P.A.U., Hyderabad.

Vyas, N.N. (1970) 'Women in Tribal Society', Tribe, Vol. VII. No.3, p. 25.

Walia, B.N.S. et.al (1974) 'Breast feeding and Learning practices in an urban population', *Indian Pediatrics*, Vol, XI, No.2, pp. 133-136.

Waterlow, J.L. (1981) 'Observation on the suckling dilemma—a personal view'. *J. of Human Nutrition*, Vol. 35, pp. 165-172.

Waterlow, J.L. and Thomson, A. M. (1979) 'Observation on the adequacy of breast feeding', Lance, 2; p. 238.

Whiting, B.B. and Whiting, J.W.M. (1975) Children of six cultures: A Psycho-cultural Analysis, Cambridge, Massachusetts: Harvard Unit Press.

Woodruff, C.W. (1978) The Science of Infant Nutrition and the art of infant feeding *JAMA*, Vol. 24, No.7, p.657.

Wyon, J.B. and Gordon, J.E. (1971) 'The Khanna Study' Harvard university Press, Cambridge.

Yadav, K.S. (1968) 'Gond Cross-cousin marriages' *Man in India*, Vol, 48, No.4, pp. 345-346.

Yaseen Saheb, S. and Ananda Bhanu, B. (1984) 'Consanguinity among the Irular of Tamil Nadu', *Indian Anthropologist*, Vol. 14, No.2, pp. 133-143.

Index